GCSE Mathematics

GCSE Mathematics 9-1 Targeting Grades 7, 8 and 9 Book 2

Barton Maths Tuition

Copyright © 2017 Barton Maths Tuition

GCSE Mathematics 9-1 Targeting Grades 7, 8 and 9 by Barton Maths Tuition.

Published by Amazon Kindle Direct Publishing.

All rights reserved. No portion of this book may be reproduced in any form, stored in any retrieval system, or transmitted in any form by any means – electronic, mechanical, photocopy, recording or otherwise – without permission from the author, except as permitted by U.K. copyright law.

Cover by Thomas Bennett and Julia Sands.

ISBN: 9781973246107

GCSE Mathematics 9 – 1

GCSE questions targeted at levels 7 – 9.

Barton Maths Tuition

This book is designed to provide students with an insight into how to tackle the tougher questions presented on the GCSE Mathematics Papers. The questions focus on strategy and technique rather than repetition as would normally be found in an exercise book.

The book is divided broadly into five sections (Algebra, Ratio, Number Crunching, Geometry and Probability) with some overlap between topics. The majority of the grade 7 and above questions require skills from several areas of GCSE mathematics.

The questions focus on key areas that students frequently require assistance with. These topics include:

1. The use of proportion.
2. Recognising an algebra based question.
3. Selecting appropriate solution strategies.

The full solutions are given at the end of the book. It is recommended that the solutions are studied carefully and that students take note of the methods used to solve the problems. There are over 100 questions in the book. Some of the questions are quite challenging even for the most able GCSE student. This book by itself will cover some, but not all, of the topics encountered on the GCSE syllabus. There will be other books available in the series that seek to cover the other topics.

CONTENTS

	Acknowledgments	vii
1	Algebra	1
2	Ratio	11
3	Number Crunching	14
4	Geometry	24
5	Probability	34
6	Algebra Solutions	36
7	Ratio Solutions	61
8	Number Crunching Solutions	66
9	Geometry Solutions	84
10	Probability Solutions	102

ACKNOWLEDGMENTS

The author wishes to thank Julia Sands for providing the illustrations and for editing this book.

1 ALGEBRA

1

A rectangle is split into two triangles and a hexagon.
The rectangle has side lengths 12cm and 10cm.
The ratio of the areas of the shapes formed, A, B and C is 1:3:2 respectively.
Find the values of the unknown lengths x and y.

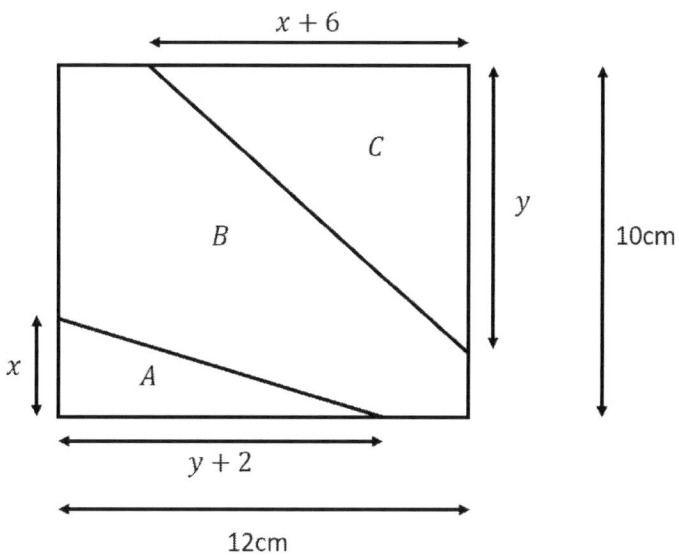

2

If $4^x = 8^{2x+2}$, what is the value of 9^x?

3

Find the value of a in the identity:
$5x^2 - 40x + 8 \equiv ax^2 + 2(bx + c)^2$

4

Solve the simultaneous equations:
$2^x = 4^y$
$x^2 = 12y$

Algebra

5

A triangle, ABC is shown formed from the y-axis and two lines in the diagram.
The diagram is not to scale.
The lines have equations $y = 3x + 2$ and $y = -5x + 26$
What is the area of triangle ABC?
Show how you decide.

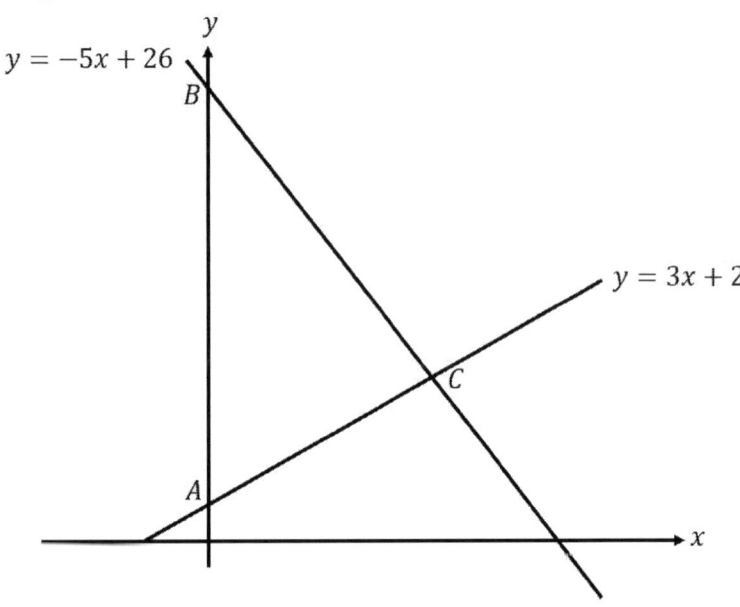

6

A car and a motorbike are racing on a circuit.
They both start from the same start point.
The car is given a 5-second head start before the motorbike.
The velocity-time graph below shows how the race progressed.
The equation of the car line is given by $V = 2.5t$.
The equation of the motorbike line is given by $V = 10t - 50$.
At what time did the motorbike overtake the car?

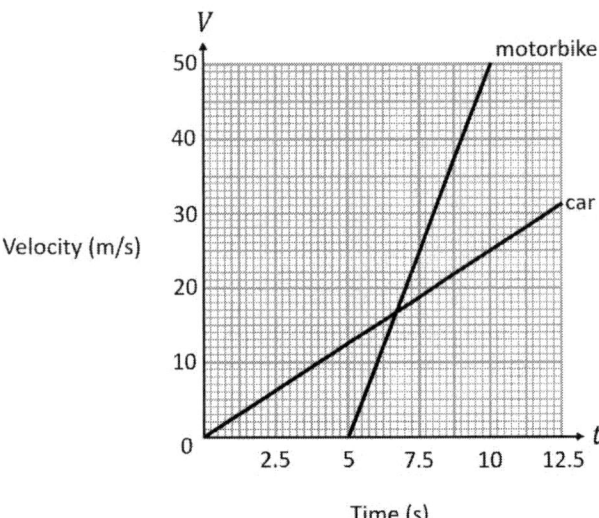

GCSE Mathematics 9 – 1

7

A golf ball is struck and the trajectory of the golf ball can be modelled by a quadratic curve of the form $y = ax^2 + bx + c$. The x and y values are in metres.
The point that the golf ball started its flight from is the origin.
When the golf ball is 80m horizontally from the origin, it reaches a maximum height of 64m.
The golf ball passes through a point 150m horizontally and 15m vertically from the origin.
Find the values of a, b and c.

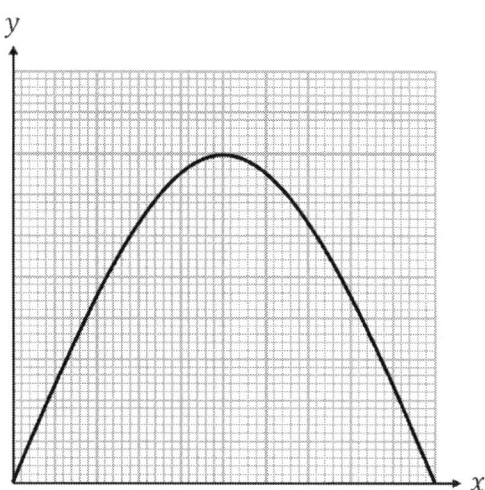

8

A lake is drying out in the summer temperatures.
The percentage decrease in surface area of the lake each day is directly proportional to the square of the temperature in degrees Celsius for that day.
At the start of the summer the lake has an area of 100km².
After one day at 40°C the lake decreases in area by 8 percent.
The percentages refer to the area of the lake at the start of the day.
What will the area of the lake be after another day of 40°C and further day of 30°C?

9

A cardboard box is to be assembled.
The box will be in the shape of a cuboid.
One of the sides must be 5cm.
The volume of the cuboid must not exceed 175cm³.
The surface area of all the faces of the cuboid must be greater than 76cm².
Given the dimensions of the cuboid shown in the diagram, find the range of values that x can take.

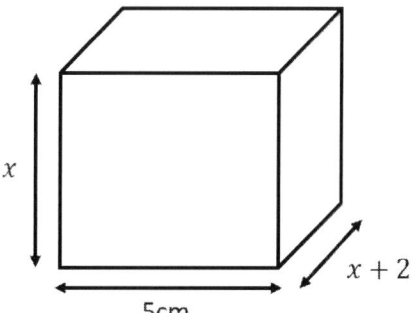

Algebra

10

Three generations of the same family are comparing their ages.
They are the son, the father and the grandfather.
The father says that he is 250% the age of the son.
The grandfather says that in four years' time he will be three times the age of the son.
The grandfather also says that he is 20 years older than the father is now.
Find the ages of the three family members at the present time.

11

When a bank account is opened customers have a choice of being contacted by post or by email.
10% of customers decide to be contacted by post and the rest decide to be contacted by email.
The bank must spend £1.50 per customer who is contacted by post and x pence per customer who is contacted by email.
The bank has 800,000 customers
The bank spends a total of £480,000 on contacting customers by post and by email.
Find the value of x.

12

A supermarket offers a points system to customers to encourage them to return to the supermarket.
For each purchase, a customer is awarded a fixed amount of points.
Extra points are then earned at a constant rate proportional to the amount a customer spends.
A shopper has spent £15 in the supermarket and has accumulated 40 points.
Another shopper has spent £25 in the supermarket and accumulated 60 points.
Find a formula that connects the amount of points earned y with the amount spent £x.

13

A ferry departs from a port.
The ferry must have no more than 100 cars on board.
The ferry must have no more than 200 passengers on board.
The total number of cars and passengers must be at least 250.
By calling the number of cars x and the number of passengers y, show these requirements as a set of inequalities and shade the region that is satisfied by the inequalities.

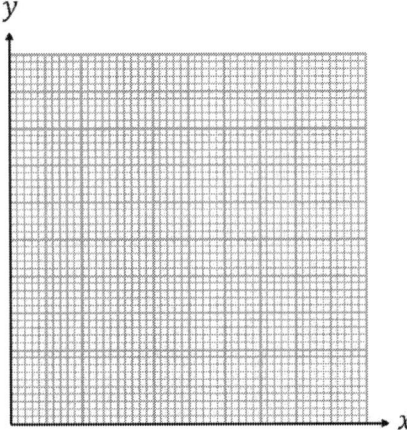

GCSE Mathematics 9 – 1

14

Two number machines are shown below.
A number x is input into both machines.
Find the range of values of x for which four times the output of Machine A is greater than 3 times the output of Machine B.

Machine A:

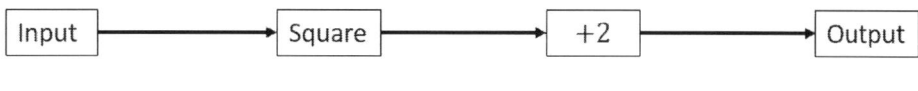

Machine B:

15

A curve with equation $y = (x-3)^2$ is shown by the graph below.
Point B is the turning point of the curve and point A is the point where the curve crosses the y-axis.
AB and AC are straight lines that are perpendicular to each other.
Find the equation of the line AC.

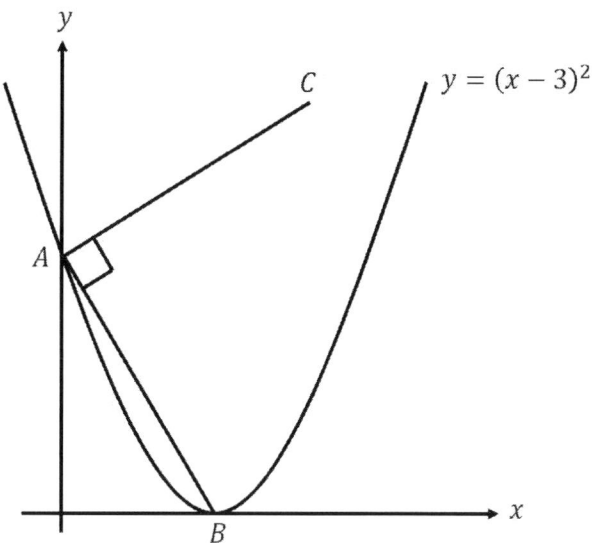

16

A sequence begins:
$3, \quad 3^3, \quad 3^5, \quad 3^7$
Show that the difference between the 14th and 15th term is equal to eight times the 14th term.

Algebra

17

Some students obtain data on the rate of retreat of a cliff face and the height of the cliff.
Their results are shown in the graph below.
Make a suggestion as to the formula that connects the rate of retreat R and the height h of the cliff.

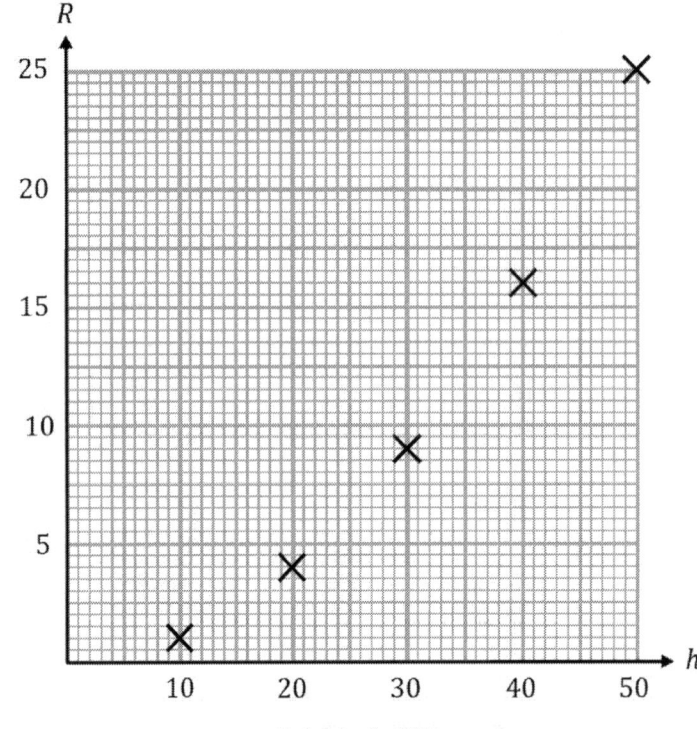

Rate of retreat in metres per year

Height of cliff in metres

18

A millionaire decides to give half of all his wealth away at the end of the year.
The millionaire then decides to give half of all his wealth away at the end of the second year.
e.g. after one year he gives half his wealth away, then at the end of the second year he gives away half of what he had at the end of the first year.
After five years the millionaire has given away £7,750,000.
What amount did the millionaire have at the start before any of the wealth was given away?

19

A family are going on holiday.
A route planner states that the journey will be 192 miles.
While travelling to the holiday destination the family encounter congestion on the motorway.
The family are travelling in the congested traffic for 42 miles.
The mean speed whilst travelling in congestion is x mph.
The mean speed of the journey whilst not in congestion is 50 mph.
The entire journey takes 5 hours.
Find the value of x.

20

The function $f(x)$ is a quadratic of the form $f(x) = x^2 + bx + c$ and is symmetric about the line $x = 2$.
The quadratic also goes through the origin.
Find the values of b and c.

GCSE Mathematics 9 – 1

21

A revision guide is on sale in two formats.
The revision guide is sold as a paperback book or as an ebook available online only.
A survey is conducted on the number of people who bought the book, what format the book was in, and whether it was for a year 10 or a year 11 student.
3,000 ebooks were sold to year 11 students which represented half of the Total copies sold.
40% of the year 11 students were sold a paperback.
Equal numbers of year 10 students bought ebooks and paperbacks.
Find the value of x shown in the frequency tree.

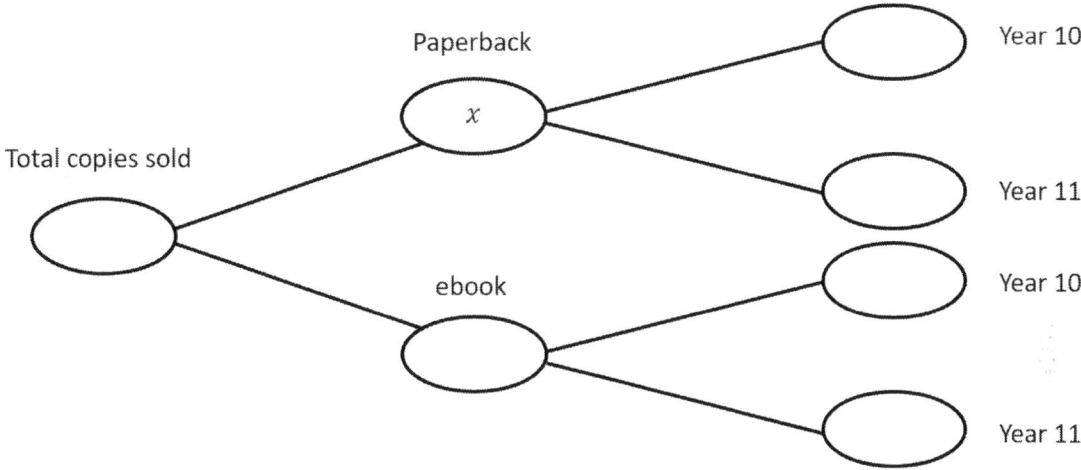

22

The force an object exerts on the ground is directly proportional to the volume of the object.
A solid cylinder is placed with its flat face on the ground.
This cylinder exerts a force on the ground and a resulting pressure.
Another solid cylinder with twice the radius and twice the height is stacked onto the first cylinder.
How many times will the pressure increase on the table when this second cylinder is added to the first?

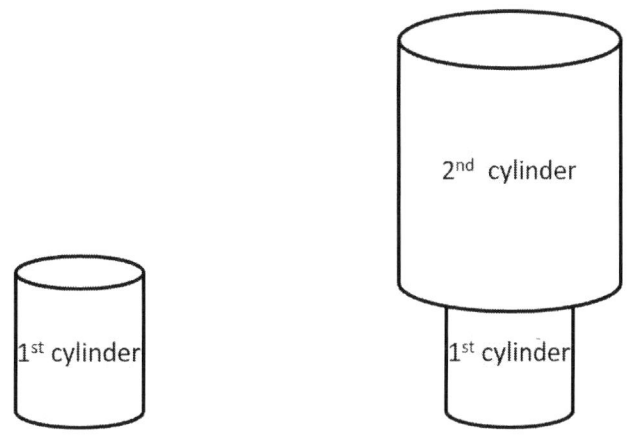

23

Solve for x:
$$\frac{5}{x+2} + \frac{8}{x+6} = 2.25$$

Algebra

24

A pattern of trapezia is shown below
Shape 1 has parallel sides of length 2cm and 4cm, and a height of 1cm.
Shape 2 has parallel sides of length 2cm and 6cm, and a height of 2cm.
The pattern continues with the longer parallel side increasing by 2cm and the height increasing by 1cm.
The areas of each trapezia form a sequence.
Find a formula for the nth term for the area of each shape formed.

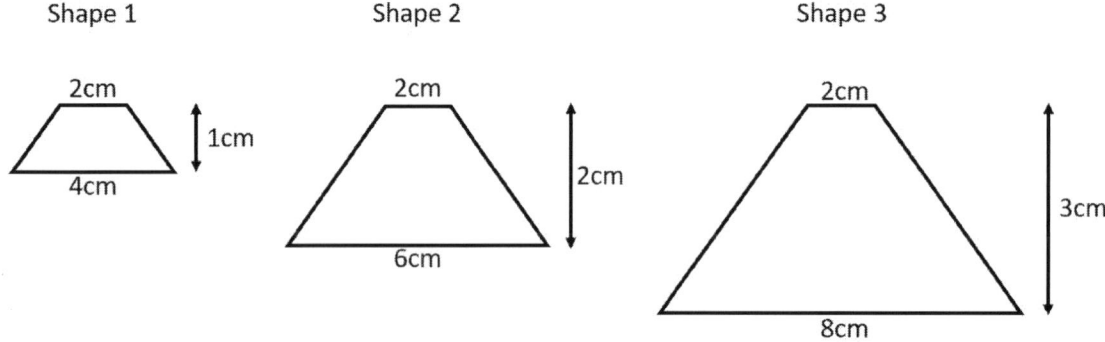

25

A sphere has radius r cm and surface area given by $4\pi r^2$.
A solid cylinder also has radius r cm and height 10cm
For what values of r is the surface area of the sphere greater than the total surface area of the cylinder?

26

An ice cube is melting.
When the surface area of the cube is 216cm² the temperature is 2°C.
The surface area of the cube is thought to be inversely proportional to the square of the temperature.
Find the ratio of the surface area of the cube at 2°C to the surface area of the cube at 6°C.
Give your ratio in its simplest form.

27

A regular octagon of side length 10cm is shown in the diagram.
A circle of radius r is shown inside the octagon with all sides of the octagon a tangent to the circle.
Show that the circle occupies $\frac{\pi r}{40}$ of the area of the octagon.

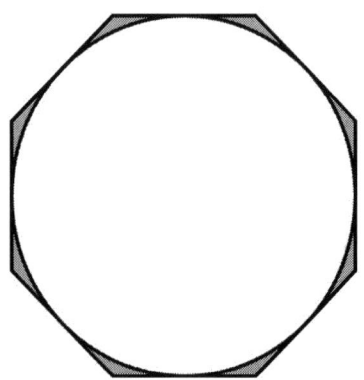

GCSE Mathematics 9 – 1

28

A radio mast is to be constructed on horizontal ground.
The radio mast will be a vertical column of height h metres.
The radio mast is held in position by metal wires.
The length l of metal wires required is proportional to the square root of the height of the radio mast.
A radio mast of height 196 metres requires 70 metres of wire.
How many metres of extra wire would be required if the height of the radio mast was increased to 256 metres?

29

A regular polygon has exterior angles that are all less than $10°$.
This regular polygon has interior angles that are all less than $175°$.
The polygon has n sides.
Between what values would n lie?

30

A parachute is designed to reduce the velocity of a falling object.
A manufacturer states that the parachute must be deployed no later than 2,000m above the ground to ensure a safe landing.
The parachute is designed to reduce the velocity of a falling object by $x\%$ every 500m.
For example, the velocity at 1,000m will be $x\%$ lower than it was at 1,500m.
If an object has a velocity of Vm/s when it is 2,000m above the ground, write a formula for the velocity Sm/s in terms of V and x for when the object lands on the ground.

31

Student A and Student B each think of a number.
Student A says that if you square his number and add 5 it will be the same as if you squared Student B's number and subtracted 6.
Student B says that the sum of both numbers is 11.
What are the two numbers?

32

A long-distance runner is competing in a race.
The runner travels at 4m/s for 360 seconds and then accelerates at a constant rate for 10 seconds.
At the end of the 10 seconds of acceleration the race is complete.
The runner travels a total distance of 1,500m.
What was the long-distance runner's final speed?

Algebra

33

Two box plots are shown below.
A student must analyse the information in the box plots even though no scale has been provided.
The student does know some facts about the box plots:
- The interquartile range of Box Plot A is 11 more than the interquartile range on Box Plot B.
- The range of Box Plot A is 32 more than the range of Box Plot B.
- The distance from the upper quartile to the maximum value of Box Plot A is 20.
- The distance from the minimum value to the lower quartile of Box Plot A is 21.
- The range of Box Plot B is 3.5 times the interquartile range of Box Plot B.

Find the range of Box Plot B.

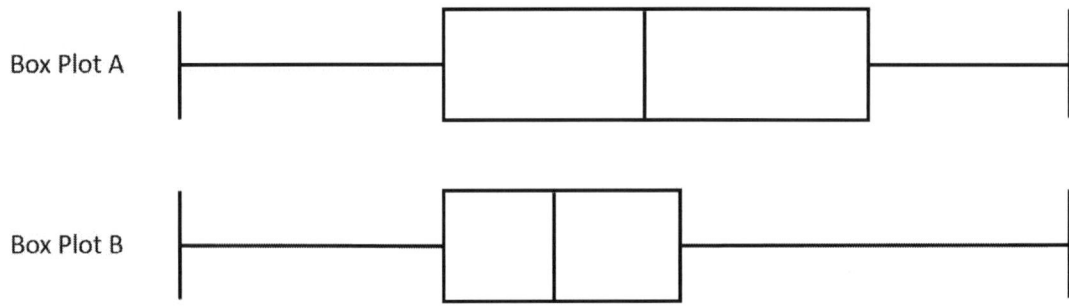

34

A frequency tree is shown below.
The frequency tree shows a survey on the type of mobile phone ownership people have.
The two types of ownership are "contract" and "pay as you go".
Of these two categories, the people were asked whether they were satisfied with their current agreement.
Five times as many people on contract were not satisfied as the people not satisfied on pay as you go.
$\frac{9}{10}$ of the people on pay as you go were satisfied with their current agreement.
$\frac{3}{4}$ of the people in the survey were on contract agreements.
252 more people were satisfied with their current agreement than those who were not satisfied with their current agreement.
Complete the frequency tree.

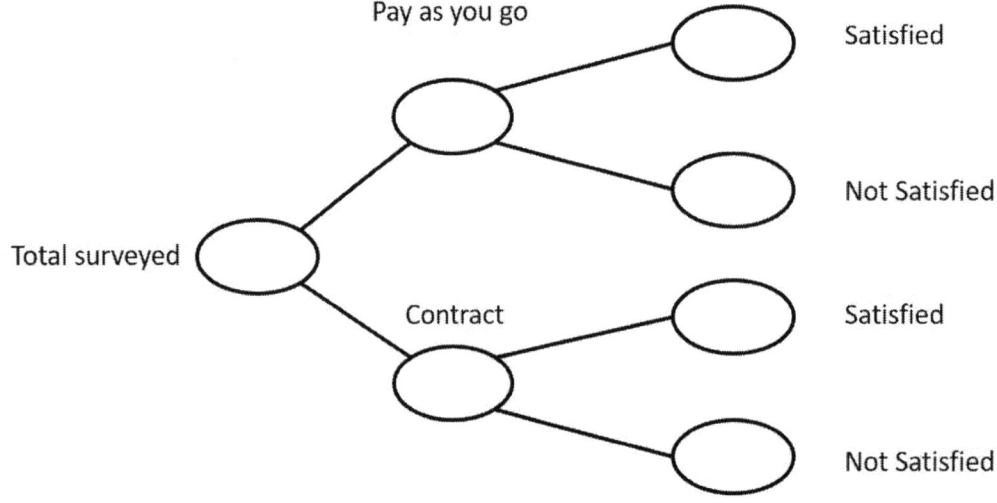

GCSE Mathematics 9 – 1

2 RATIO

1

A circle and a system of lines is shown.
The lines AB and AG are tangents to the circle and C is a point on the tangent AG.
The points B, D, E, F and G all lie on the circumference of the circle.
The angle $BEF = 70°$ and the angle $FBC = 22°$.
Angle $BDF = y$ and angle $BAC = x$.
Show that the ratio of $y : x$ is $5 : 3$.

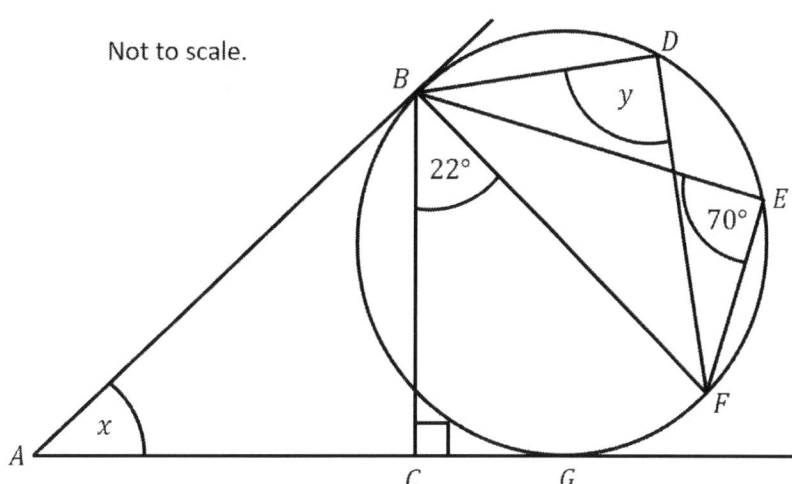

2

A parallelogram has longer side length l and shorter side length w.
The perpendicular height of the parallelogram is h.
The ratio of $l : w = 3 : 2$.
The ratio of $w : h = 2 : \sqrt{3}$.
Given that $h = 20\sqrt{3}$cm, find the area of the parallelogram.
Give your answer as a simplified surd.

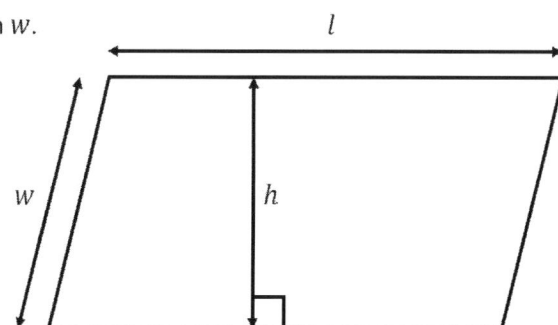

Ratio

3

A hemisphere and a cylinder have the same volume.
Both the hemisphere and the cylinder have the same radius, r.
The cylinder has height h.
Find the ratio of $r : h$.
You are given that the volume of a sphere is $volume = \frac{4}{3}\pi r^3$.

4

Two mixtures are being poured into a tank.
Mixture A is composed of water and syrup in the ratio 5:1.
Mixture B is composed of water and syrup in the ratio 8:1.
600cm³ of Mixture A have been poured into the tank.
An unknown volume, Vcm³ of Mixture B have been poured into the tank.
The tank now has water and syrup in the ratio 6:1.
Find the value of V.

5

The speed of a bird decreases at a rate of 10% every second.
The speed of an insect decreases at a rate of 70% every second.
After three seconds both the bird and the insect are travelling at the same speed.
What is the ratio of the initial speed of the bird to the initial speed of the insect?

6

The cone shown has a height h and a radius r.
The volume of the cone is 720πcm³.
The ratio of the radius to the height is $r : h = 1 : 10$
Find the value of h.
You are given that the volume of a cone is: $volume = \frac{1}{3}\pi r^2 h$.

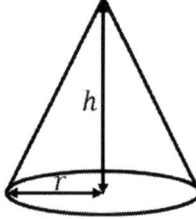

7

A set of data is found to have the following properties:
- The distance between the lower quartile and the median is twice the distance between the minimum value and the lower quartile.
- The distance between the upper quartile and the median is twice the distance between the median and the lower quartile.
- The distance between the maximum value and the upper quartile is twice the distance between the upper quartile and the median.

Find the ratio of the range to the interquartile range giving your answer in its simplest form.

GCSE Mathematics 9 – 1

8

A container is being filled with liquid.
The container is formed from an inverted cone and a cylinder.
The radius of the cone and the radius of the cylinder are the same and fit perfectly.
The liquid flows into the container at a constant rate.
If the cylinder part takes four times as long to fill as the cone part, what is the ratio of the height of the cylinder to the height of the cone?

You are given that the volume of a cone is $\frac{1}{3}\pi r^2 h$.

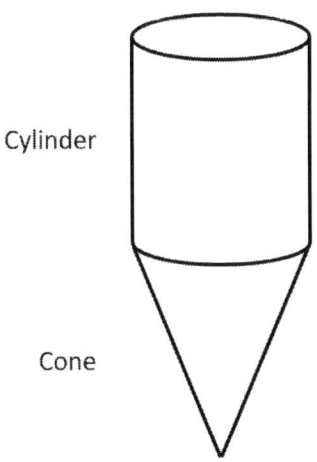

9

A cone, a sphere and a cylinder all have the same density.
The cone, the sphere and the cylinder all have a radius of 3cm.
The cone and the cylinder have a height of 12cm.
What is the ratio of their masses in the form cone : sphere : cylinder.

The volume of a cone is given by $\frac{1}{3}\pi r^2 h$.

The volume of a sphere is given by $\frac{4}{3}\pi r^3$.

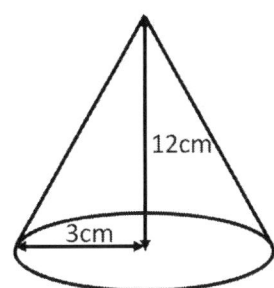 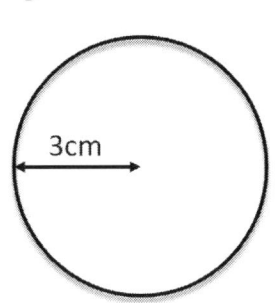 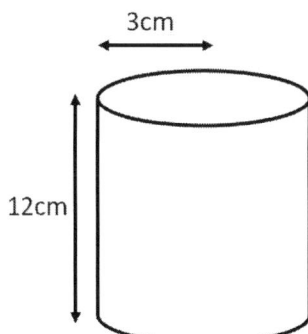

3 NUMBER CRUNCHING

1

A set of five whole numbers have the following properties:
- The range of the numbers is 17.
- The median is a multiple of 7 and equal to the mode.
- The largest number is four times as large as the second smallest number.
- The mean is 11.2.
- Two of the numbers are prime.

What are the five numbers?

2

The government has decided to change the way that income tax is calculated.
At present income tax is calculated according to the table given below:

Band	Taxation rate
Personal allowance	0% for your first £11,500
Standard rate	20% on everything between £11,500 - £45,000

The government has decided that a person earning £32,000 per year should pay the same amount of tax in the new system as they did in the old system.
If the personal allowance is increased from £11,500 to £12,000, what percentage would the standard rate have to be in the new system?

3

A submarine is descending under water.
For every 10m the submarine descends the pressure of the water increases by 1 atmosphere.
The atmosphere is measured to the nearest 0.1.
(The atmosphere is a unit of pressure.)
The depth and the pressure are directly proportional.
If the pressure increases to above 50 atmospheres, the submarine will implode.
What is the maximum safe depth that the submarine can descend to and be absolutely sure it will not implode?
Give your answer to the nearest metre.
Assume the water pressure is zero atmospheres at the surface.

GCSE Mathematics 9 – 1

4

A bookshop contains 10,000 books to the nearest 1,000.
Each book contains 400 pages to the nearest 100.
Each page contains 350 words to the nearest 10.
If a person can read 400 words per minute, what is the minimum time it would take for that person to read all the books in the bookshop?
Give your answer to the nearest hour.

5

An energy company is advising its customers to have a new energy efficient boiler installed in their homes.
The installation will cost £1,600.
The cost for gas is 3p per unit and there is a daily standing charge of 30p for an old boiler.
A family use 10,000 units of gas per year with the old boiler.
The new boiler uses 80% of the units that an old boiler would use in a year.
If you install a new boiler the daily standing charge is reduced to 25p but the cost per unit increases to 3.1p.
The energy company claims that you will have saved the cost of the installation with cheaper bills in under 20 years.
Confirm whether this claim is true or not (ignore leap years).

6

A single car tyre of a fully loaded car is in contact with the ground.
The part of the tyre in contact with the ground can be considered as a rectangle.
The force on the ground from the tyre is 4,000 newtons.
The area of the tyre in contact with the ground has dimensions 0.1m x 0.2m.
Some people get out of the car and the force on the ground from the tyre decreases to 3,200N.
The pressure on the ground remains the same.
What must the new area in contact with the ground be?

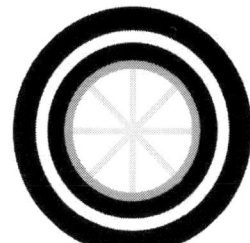

7

Information about two countries is shown in the table below.
There is information on the area of the country and the number of doctors.

	Country A	Country B
Area (km²) nearest 100km²	670,000	1,115,200
Total doctors to nearest 100	23,100	38,500

A geography student says that Country A must definitely have more doctors per square kilometre than Country B.
Determine whether this statement is correct.

Number Crunching

8

A goldfish bowl is made in the shape of a hollow glass sphere of radius 15cm.
The goldfish bowl is completely filled with water.
The density of both goldfish bowl and water combined is 1.1g/cm³.
There are 12kg of water in the goldfish bowl.
The volume of glass in the goldfish bowl is 1420cm³.
Find the density of the glass used to make the goldfish bowl.
Give your answer to three significant figures.
The volume of a sphere is given by $\frac{4}{3}\pi r^3$.

9

The temperature of a greenhouse increases throughout the day.
At 8a.m. the temperature of the greenhouse is 10°C.
This temperature rises 5°C every hour for 10 hours before it begins to cool again.
When the greenhouse is cooling the temperature falls by 20% of its temperature at the start of the hour every hour.
What is the temperature of the greenhouse at 11p.m.?
Give your answer to the nearest 0.1°C.

10

On a regular 12 numbered clock, how many degrees would the minute hand turn between the times of 2hrs 26 minutes 36 seconds and 3hrs 22 minutes 30 seconds?
Both times are in the afternoon.

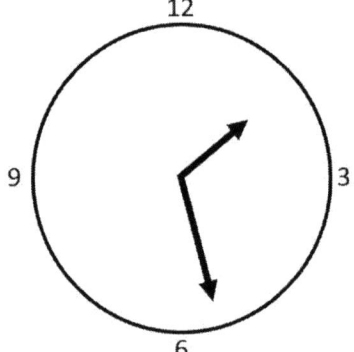 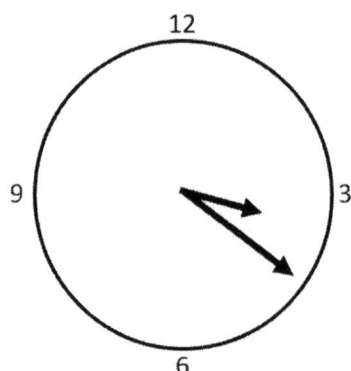

11

The cumulative frequency graph shows the grade on a 1 – 9 scale (with 9 being the highest) that students obtained in a GCSE maths exam.
Older GCSE maths papers were marked from G – A* (with A* being the highest).
A parent is trying to determine what number-grade you need to get a grade A and what number-grade you need to get a grade C to compare with older year groups.
A student says that the top 70% of the population should get grade C.
The student also says that the top 20% of the population should get grade A.
Use the cumulative frequency diagram to suggest which grade numbers relate to the grade C and grade A boundary.
You must explain your conclusions.

GCSE Mathematics 9 – 1

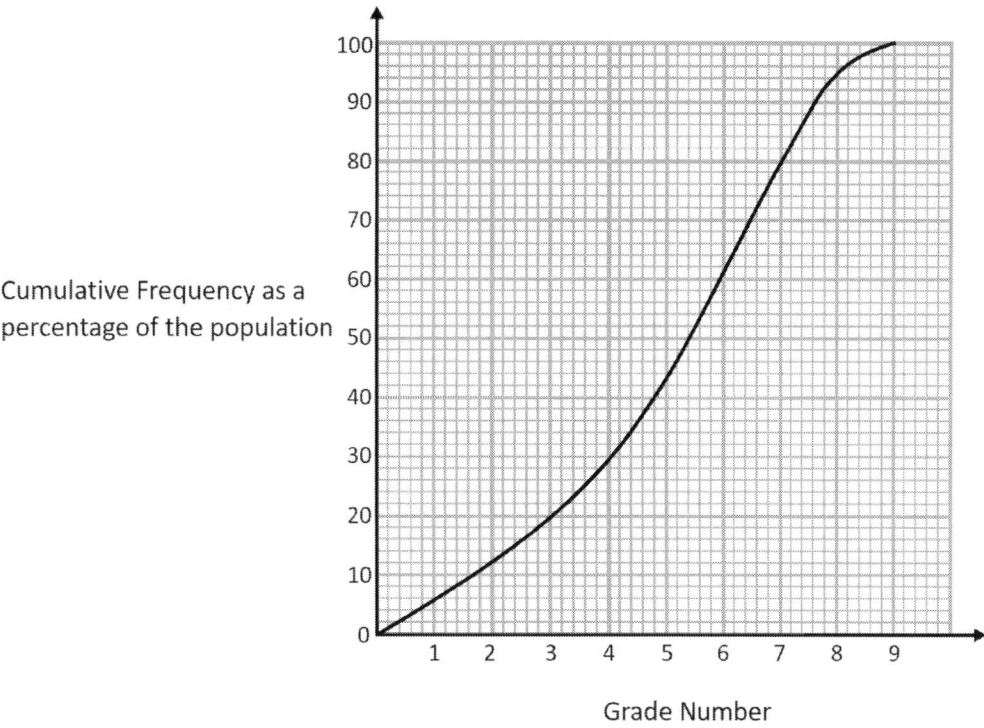

Cumulative Frequency as a percentage of the population

Grade Number

12

A maths exam is designed such that up to the top 20% of students who take the exam are awarded a level 7.
If the top 20% have all got above 55% of the total marks available then the top 10% are awarded a level 7.
If the top 20% have all got above 70% of the total marks available then the top 15% are awarded a level 7.
If the top 20% have all got above 80% of the total marks available then the top 20% are awarded a level 7.
The exam has a total of 80 marks available.
The cumulative frequency curve shows the results for a group of students.
Estimate how many students from the group achieved a level 7?

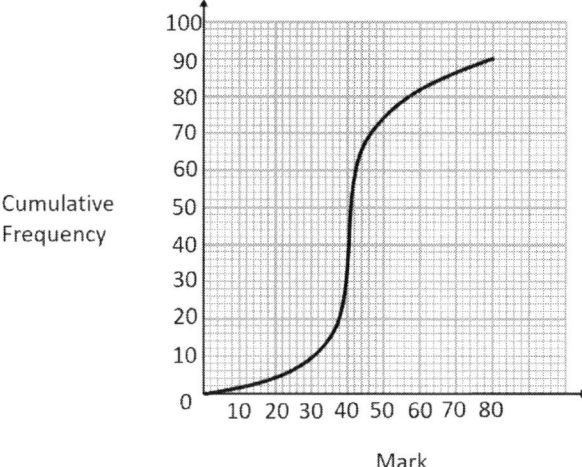

Cumulative Frequency

Mark

13

Which of the following would exert the most pressure on a horizontal flat surface?
1. A cuboid with a square face of side 20cm in contact with the surface and exerting a force of 800 newtons.
2. A cylinder of radius 80mm with the circular face in contact with the surface and exerting a force of 402 newtons.

Number Crunching

14

Two solid prisms are placed on a horizontal table.
One prism is a cylinder and the other is a trapezoidal prism.
The cylinder has height 20cm, volume 180πcm³ and exerts a force of 30 newtons on the table.
The trapezium forming the cross section of the trapezoidal prism is shown below.
The trapezoidal prism exerts a force of 17 newtons on the table.
Which prism exerts the greatest pressure on the table?

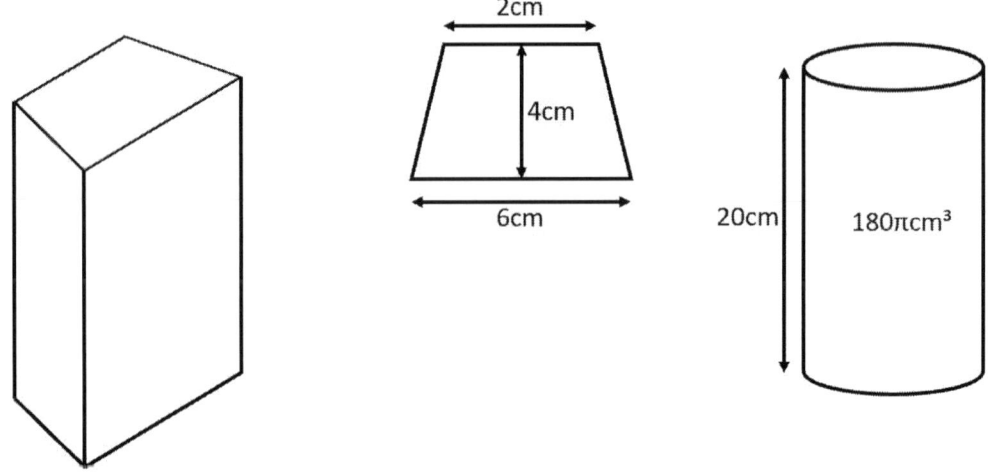

15

A government is offering an incentive scheme for those who purchase electric cars.
If a diesel car is exchanged for a new electric car the government will offer £2,500 scrappage for the diesel car and pay 20% of the purchase price of the new electric car.
The mean value of a new electric car is £28,000.
The government will fund the scheme up to a total of £500 million.
Estimate how many electric cars the scheme can be used to fund.

16

An electronics retailer offers insurance when an electrical product is purchased.
The insurance will pay out the value of the device, at that time, if it is broken beyond repair.
A typical electronic product is expected to lose 20% of its value at the start of the year every year.
e.g. an insurance company would pay out £80 for a device bought for £100 one year ago.
The price of insurance for 3 years is £150.
A device is broken beyond repair at the end of the third year.
Calculate the range of values that the original purchase price can be such that the insurance pay out exceeds the cost of the insurance cover.

17

The number of prime numbers less than 20 is multiplied by the number of odd numbers less than 48.
The number of square numbers less than 200 is raised to the power of the first positive even number.
Which of these values is the largest?

GCSE Mathematics 9 – 1

18

An artist is painting a picture.
The picture is in the shape of a rectangle and of dimensions 3m x 2m.
The paint for the picture is on sale:
Red paint costs 58p per square inch of painting.
Other paint colours cost 45p for every 10cm² of painting.
The artist estimates that 8% of the area of the picture will be red paint and the rest will be other paint colours.
Calculate the cost to complete the painting.
1 inch is equivalent to 2.54cm.

19

A model railway has a scale of 1:76.
A model train travels at 8cm per second.
What would this speed be in miles per hour in a real full-size train?
Use the fact that 1 mile is approximately 1.6km.

20

Two types of cheese are on sale in a shop.
The first cheese is in the shape of a cylinder with a price directly proportional to the volume of the cheese.
This cheese has a radius of 4cm, a height of 10cm and a price of £10.
The second cheese is in the shape of a sphere with a price directly proportional to the surface area of the cheese.
This cheese has a surface area of 144πcm² and a price of £18.
You are given that the volume of a sphere is given by $\frac{4}{3}\pi r^3$ and the surface area of a sphere is given by $4\pi r^2$.
Which cheese would be cheaper to buy if 200cm³ of each cheese was required in the shape of a sphere.

21

A number less than 100 has the digit "one" in it.
The number is 3 units away from a square number.
Write down the median of the possible numbers that it could be.

22

An estimate for the number π is given by the following:

$$\pi \approx \sqrt[3]{40 - \sqrt{80}}$$

If the above approximation was used to calculate the area of a circle of radius 5cm, what is the percentage error compared to using the calculator value of π?
Give your answer to two significant figures.

23

Use iteration on the following formula to find the value of x correct to two decimal places starting with $x_1 = 2.5$.

$$x_{n+1} = \sqrt{3 - \frac{1}{x_n}}$$

Number Crunching

24

Two pie charts below show the proportion of people who own mobile phones and the proportion of people who own a tablet PC.
Each pie chart represents a survey of the same 100 people.
A Venn diagram is used to represent the data for the same 100 people but is incomplete.
Use the information in the pie charts to complete the Venn diagram below.

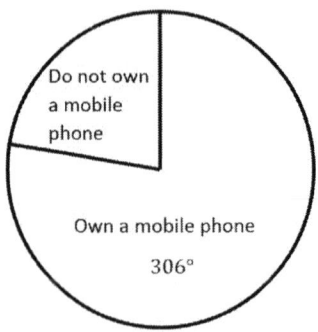
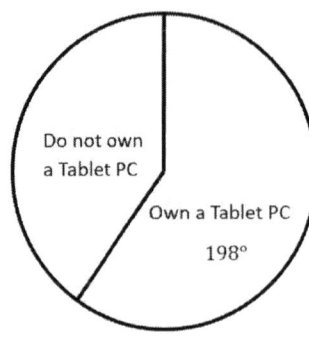
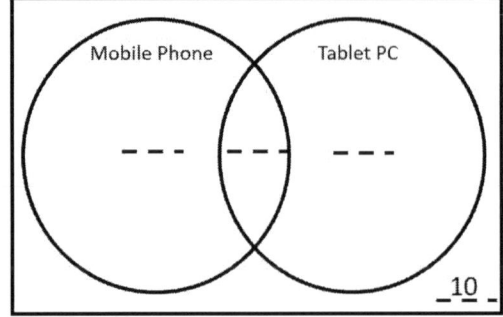

25

A weed is spreading throughout a flowerbed.
Each day, the weed grows as much as it did in the previous two days.
On day four the weed grew 11mm and on day six the weed grew 29mm.
How far did the weed grow on day two?

26

Two types of butter have different quantities of salt:
Butter A has a salt content of 1g per 50g of butter.
Butter B has an unknown salt content.
An adult daily salt allowance is 6g.
A man has eaten 100g of Butter A.
The man can eat a further 32g of Butter B to reach the daily salt allowance.
How many grams of salt per 50 grams of butter does Butter B contain?

27

A sundial is used to tell the time.
The sundial reads a time of 13:00 correct to an unknown level of accuracy.
Later the sundial reads a time of 20:00 correct to the nearest two hours.
The shortest time that could have elapsed between the two times is five and three-quarter hours.
What level of accuracy was the 13:00 time given to?

28

A pilot of a plane has two choices as to how far his plane can travel.
The plane can travel at 200mph or the plane can travel at 400mph.
The fuel consumption is 50% greater when the plane travels at 400 mph.
If the plane can travel 480 miles at 200mph how many miles can it travel at 400mph?
The plane always starts with the same amount of fuel.

GCSE Mathematics 9 – 1

29

A professor sets his students a test with a score out of 50.
The professor believes he can predict how his students will perform in the test.
The professor claims three things:
- The median will be 26 or 27.
- The number of students scoring below 20% will be the same as students scoring 80% or above.
- The range will be 50.

Here is a table of results for the students:

Mark (m)	Number of students
$0 \leq m < 10$	8
$10 \leq m < 20$	16
$20 \leq m < 30$	24
$30 \leq m < 40$	24
$40 \leq m \leq 50$	8

Given the data in the table, comment on whether the claims are correct.

30

A shopping receipt shows a bill for four different items.
The items are milk, cereal, butter and eggs.
A computer error has incorrectly assigned the price of the milk.
The first table shows the true cost of three of the items.

Item	Cost
Cereal	750g for £2
Butter	500g for £2.50
Eggs	12 eggs for £1.50

The second table shows some of the information on the receipt.

Item	Quantity
Milk	4 pints
Cereal	1,500g
Butter	500g
Eggs	12 eggs
Total	£12

The receipt total is £2.40 more than it should be.
If all items had been increased by the same proportion as the milk, what would the receipt total be now?

31

A general election is to be held in a country.
80% of the population are able to vote.
Of the 80% it is expected that x% of those able to vote will actually vote.
The country has a population of 900,000 of which 504,000 actually voted.
Find the value of x.

Number Crunching

32

The bar chart shows the population of three counties in the UK given to the nearest 100,000.
If the population of Dorset is increasing at 2% per year, Worcestershire increasing by 3% per year and Cumbria increasing at 5% per year, is it possible for Cumbria to reach 1 million people first?
You must show your working.

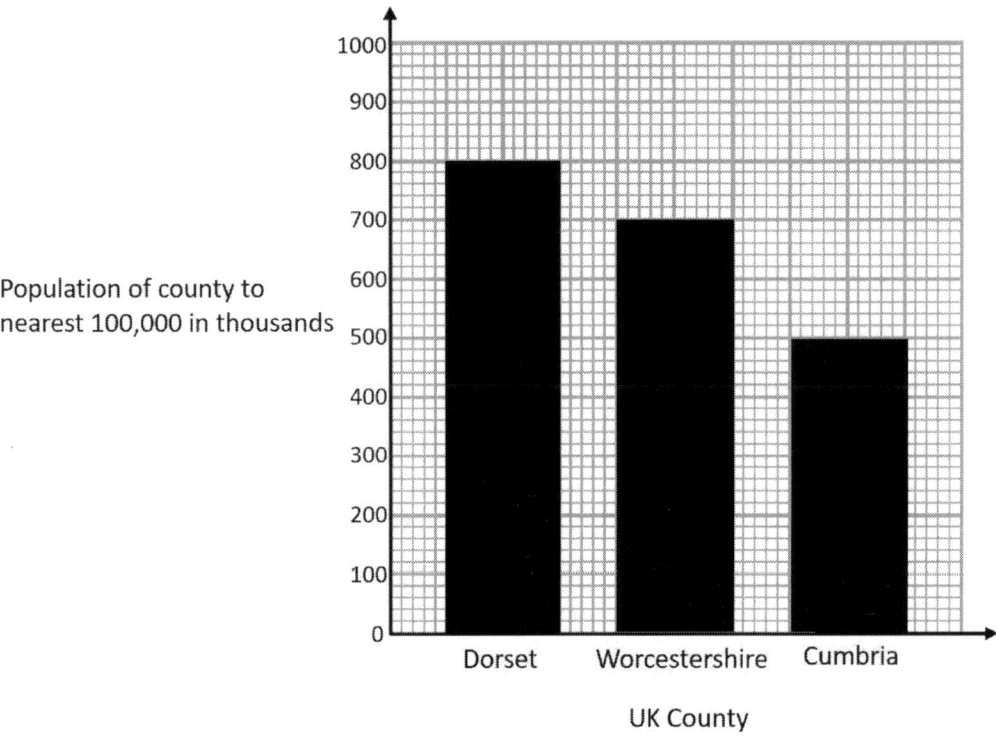

33

Five friends share a cylindrical cake out between them.
The cake is meant to be split into five equal sectors as shown in the diagram below.
Each sector is measured to the nearest degree
The first four friends take their share of the cake.
What is the smallest fraction of the cake that the fifth friend could be left with?

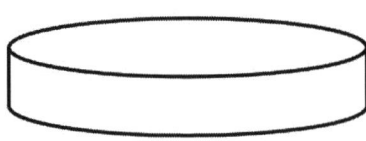
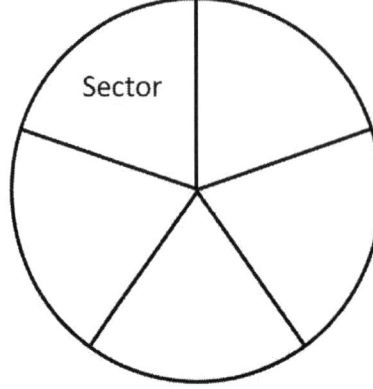

34

A manufacturer of screws is deciding what size of plastic container the screws should go in.
The screws measure 50mm in length and can be treated as a cuboid with a square face of side length 10mm.
For each screw that is sold the manufacturer makes a 2p profit.
Two types of container are proposed; both are cuboids.
Container A has dimensions 20cm x 10cm x 5cm.
Container B has dimensions 15cm x 10cm x 10cm.
There is a cost of 1p for every 50cm³ of volume to produce the containers.
If each container was completely full of screws, how much more profit does the manufacturer make on container B?

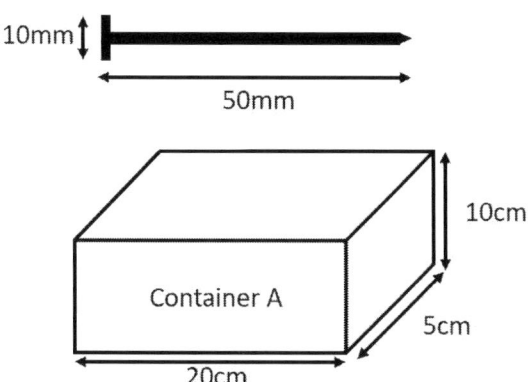
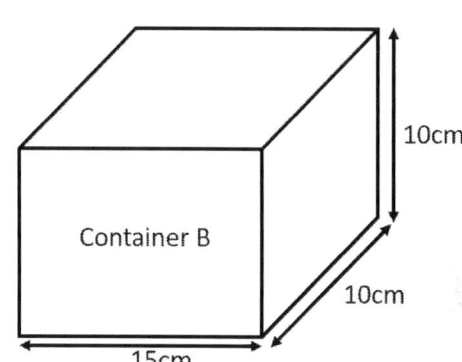

4 GEOMETRY

1

A jigsaw is to be constructed showing a map of a city.
The city has the shape of a rectangle with dimensions 12km x 10km.
The jigsaw is to be made from a piece of card that is in the shape of the circle.
The circle has radius 16cm.
Would a scale of 1:50,000 be enough to fit a scale map of the city on the card?

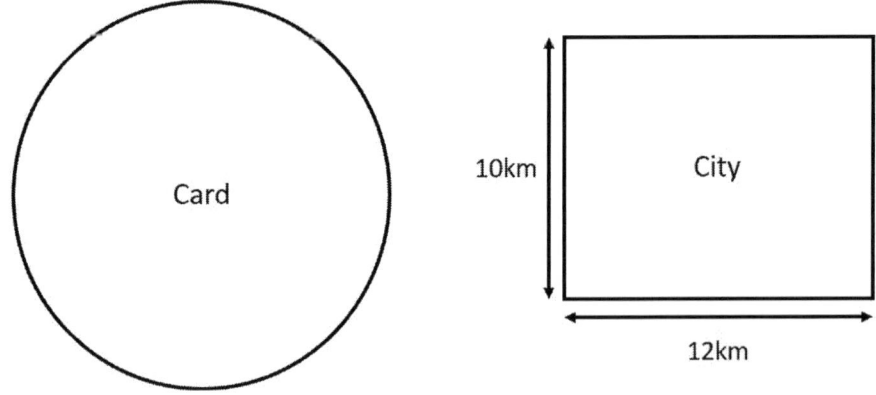

2

A bridge is to be constructed.
The bridge will be stable as long as the width between the supports is no more than 20m.
The undersection of the bridge is in the shape of a trapezium and the bridge is symmetrical about a vertical axis.
An engineer proposes the design below.
Will this design be stable?

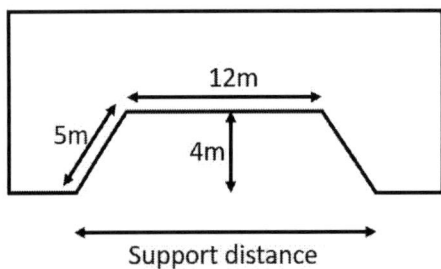

GCSE Mathematics 9 – 1

3

Use a ruler and compass only in this question.
A television mast is to be constructed such that:
- It is closer to road AB than the road AC.
- It is the same distance from A as it is to C.

Find the locus of points for the television mast.

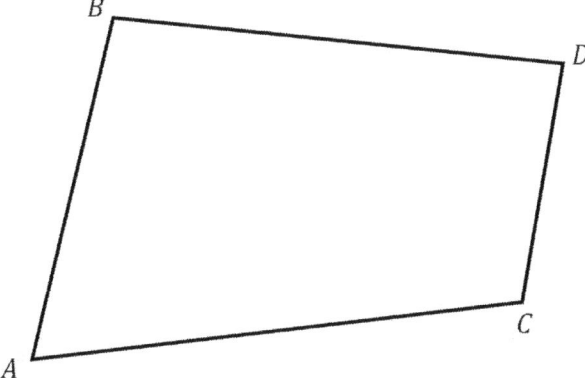

4

A shape is shown on the grid below.
Point A is at coordinates (4,4) and point B is at coordinates (5,6).
Find a single transformation such that the points A and B are invariant.

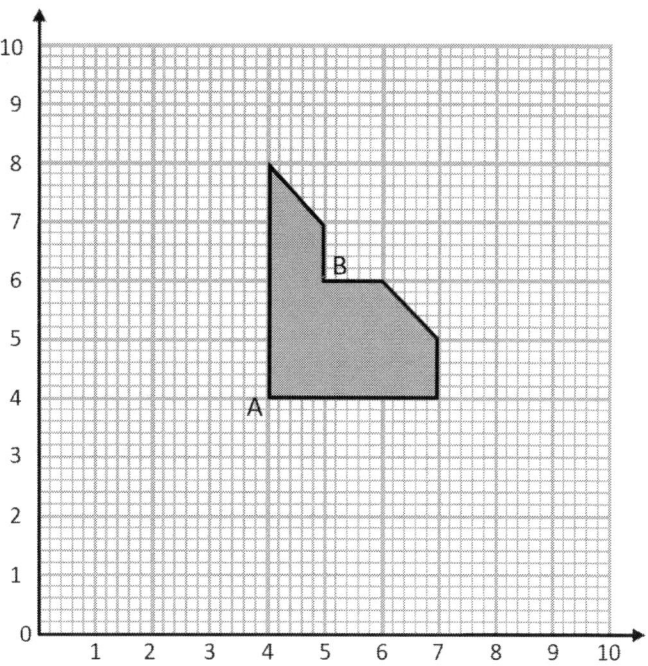

5

A road map with a scale of 1:20,000 shows a forested area.
Another tourist map with a scale of 1:50,000 shows the same forested area.
Find the ratio of the **areas** of the forested area on both maps.
Give your ratio as integers in the form of the ratio below
tourist map area : road map area

Geometry

6

The vector $\overrightarrow{AB} = \mathbf{a}$.
The vector $\overrightarrow{BC} = \mathbf{b}$.
The area of triangle ADE is 9 times the area of triangle ABC.
The lines BC and DE are parallel.
ABD and ACE are straight lines.
Find the vector $\overrightarrow{AE}$ in terms of $\mathbf{a}$ and $\mathbf{b}$.

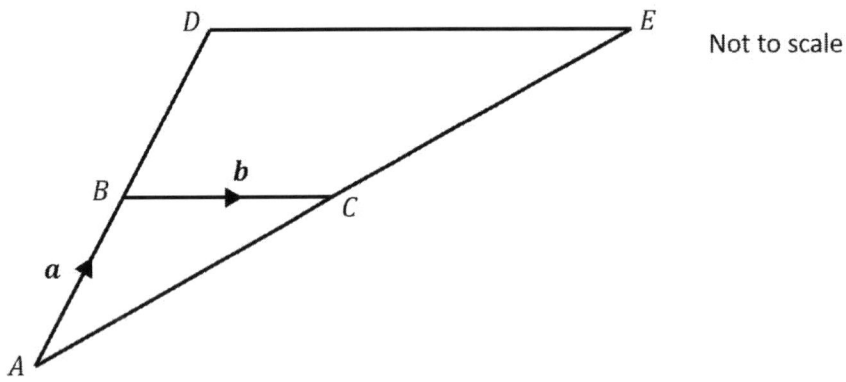

Not to scale

7

A shape has area 8cm².
The shape is rotated $180°$.
The shape is then reflected in the line $y = x$.
The shape is enlarged by scale factor 2 about the point (1,2).
The shape is translated by the vector $\binom{4}{5}$.
What is the new area of the shape?

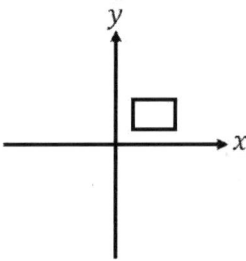

8

Two circles are shown in the diagram.
The point O is the centre of the smaller circle.
The angle BOA is $40°$.
ACD is a straight line.
BC and DE are parallel.
Find the size of angle AFE.

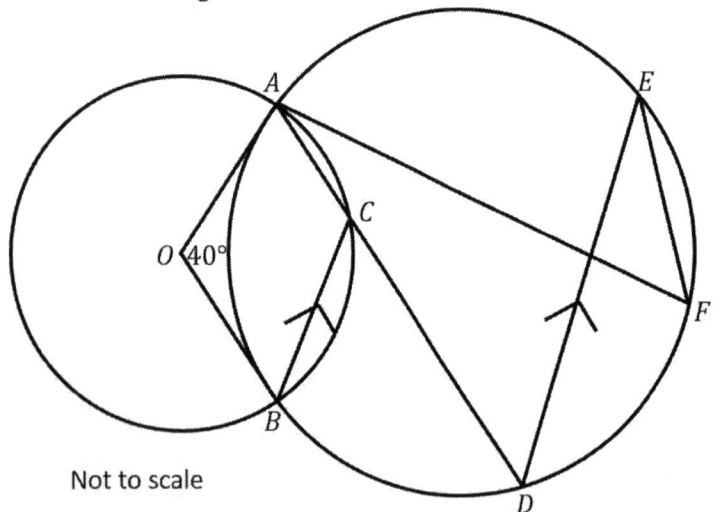

Not to scale

GCSE Mathematics 9 – 1

9

Two triangles are shown in the diagrams below.
A student claims that Triangle A has the largest area because it has the largest angle.
Both triangles have two sides of 3cm.
Find the areas of both triangles to confirm whether this claim is true.

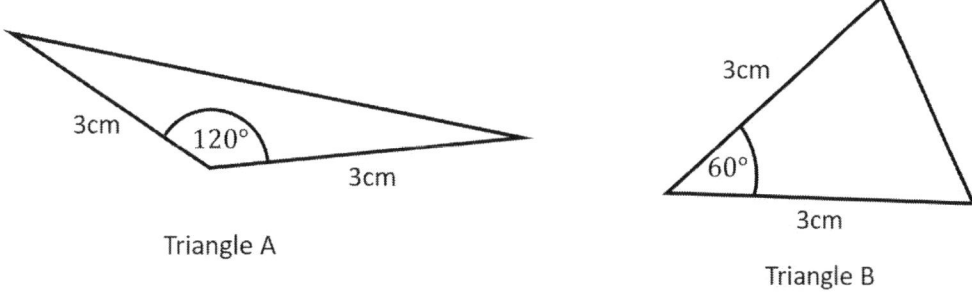

Triangle A

Triangle B

10

The graph below shows how the depth of liquid poured into a container varies with time.
The container is filled at a constant rate.
Draw a sketch of the cross section of a container that would correspond to the graph shape below.

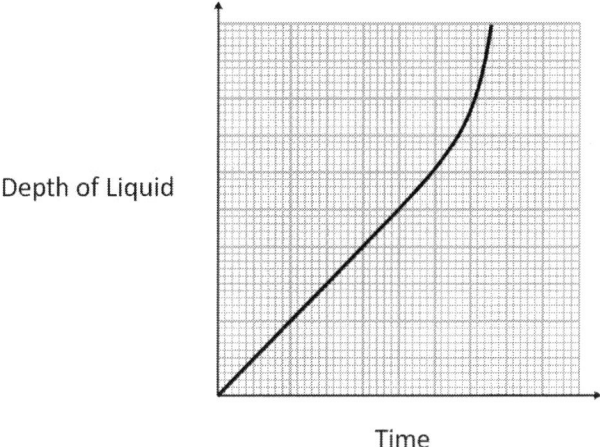

11

An ice cube is melting.
Assume that the cube shape is retained as it melts.
If the cube has lost 40% of its initial volume, what percentage of surface area has been lost?
Give your answer to the nearest percentage.

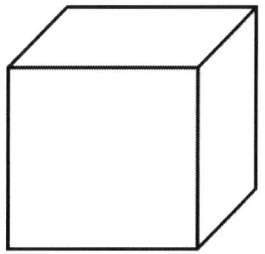

Geometry

12

A triangle ABC is shown next to an isosceles trapezium $BEDC$.
The triangle and the trapezium share a common side BC.
$AB = 5$cm, $AC = 6$cm, $BE = 10$cm, $CD = 16$cm
The trapezium has height 4cm.
Find the area of triangle ABC.

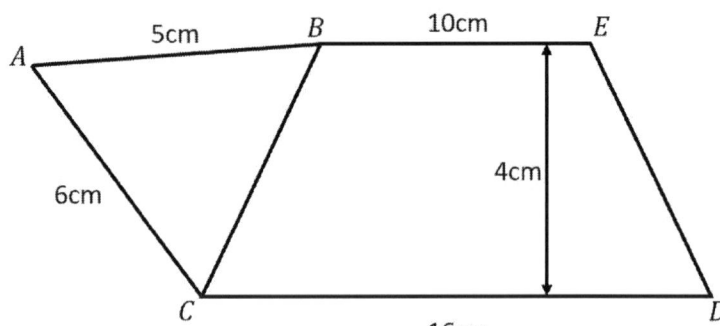

13

Two regular polygons are joined by a common side as shown in the diagram.
The diagram is not to scale.
The exterior angle of one of the polygons is 2° more than the other.
Find the number of sides of Polygon A and Polygon B.

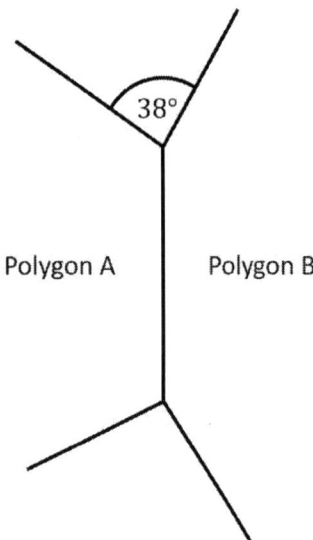

14

A map to find some buried treasure gives directions from two different locations.
The first direction is:
Starting from point A, go 3 miles east and then 4 miles north, then you have reached the treasure.
The second direction is:
Starting from point B, go 5 miles west and then 12 miles south, then you have reached the treasure.
Find the distance between the start locations A and B.
Give your answer to three significant figures.

GCSE Mathematics 9 – 1

15

A triangle ABC is shown below.
The triangle is not to scale.
Three semicircles are attached to each side of the triangle with diameters equal to the side lengths.
The area of each semicircle is shown.
Prove that triangle ABC is a right-angled triangle.

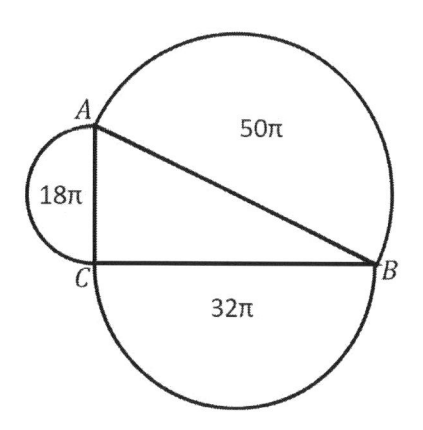

16

A hot air balloon is drifting in the wind.
The balloon begins from point A.
The balloon drifts 5 miles southeast.
It then drifts $\frac{10}{\sqrt{2}}$ miles west.
How far away is the balloon from its original start position at A?

17

A circle of radius 1cm and centre O is shown in the diagram below but not to scale.
The line ABC is a tangent to the circle.
The line DOE is a straight line.
DB and BE are chords in the circle.
OB is a radius.
Angle EBC is 15°.
Find the area of the shaded segment giving your answer to three significant figures.

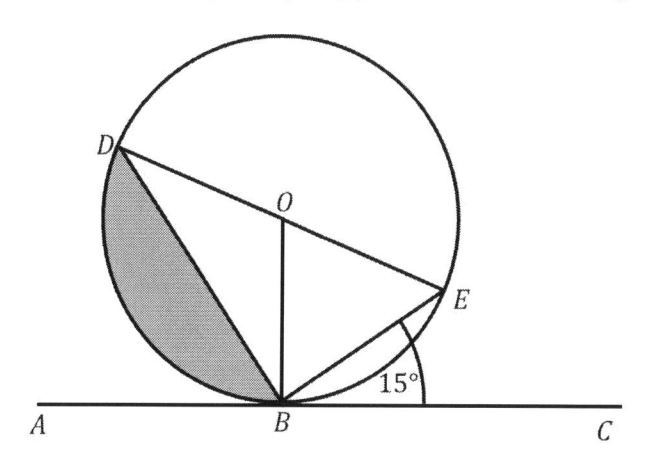

Geometry

18

An egg timer is made from two identical square-based pyramids.
One pyramid is joined to the top of the other as shown in the diagram below.
The pyramids have a square base of side 8cm and each has a vertical height of 12cm.

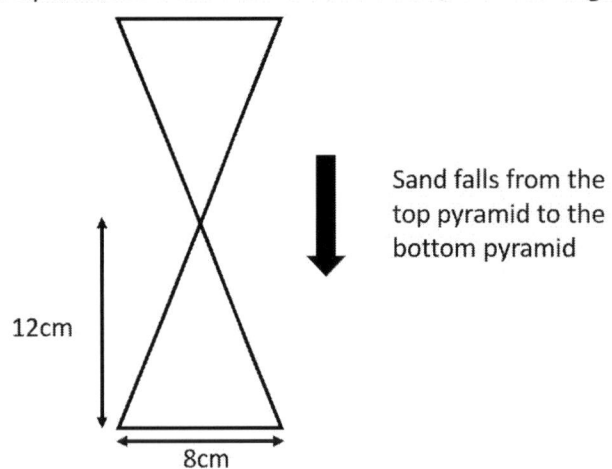

12cm

Sand falls from the top pyramid to the bottom pyramid

8cm

The pyramid at the top is filled with sand and is allowed to empty over time into the lower pyramid.
Each second 0.5cm³ of sand moves from the top pyramid into the lower pyramid.
When the top pyramid has emptied the egg timer is rotated 180 degrees and the process repeats.
The egg timer was started at 12:00 noon and a pyramid has been allowed to completely empty six times.
What time is it now to the nearest minute?

The volume of a pyramid is given by $volume = \frac{1}{3} \times base\ area \times height$.

19

A kite $ABCD$ is shown below.
Side AB = 5cm.
Side AD = 12cm.
Angle BAD is a right angle.
The lines AC and BD are the diagonals of the kite which cross at X.
Exactly how many times longer is the line DX greater than the line BX?

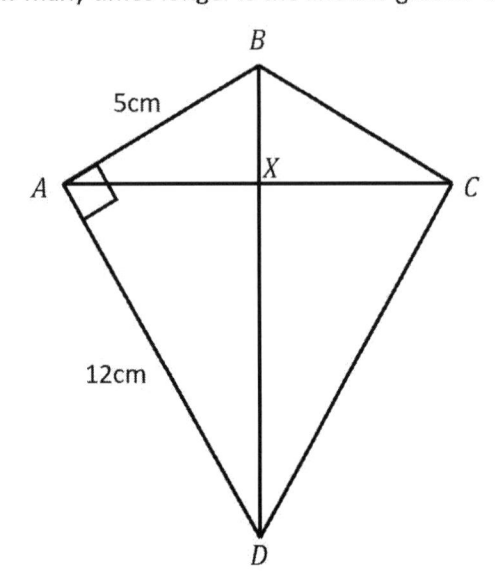

20

A cuboid is shown in the diagram below.
A triangular prism is removed from the cuboid as shown.
The triangular prism is the same length as the cuboid.
The cuboid has cross sectional side lengths of 9cm and $4\sqrt{3}$cm.
The triangular prism makes up a quarter of the entire volume of the cuboid.
Given that the triangular cross section is equilateral, find the length of one of the sides of the equilateral triangle.

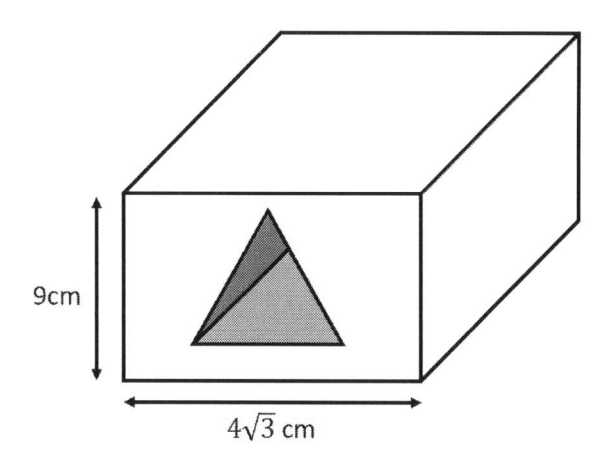

9cm

$4\sqrt{3}$ cm

21

A circle and a sector have the same area.
The radius of the circle is 5cm.
The angle of the sector is $10°$.
Find the radius, r, of the sector.

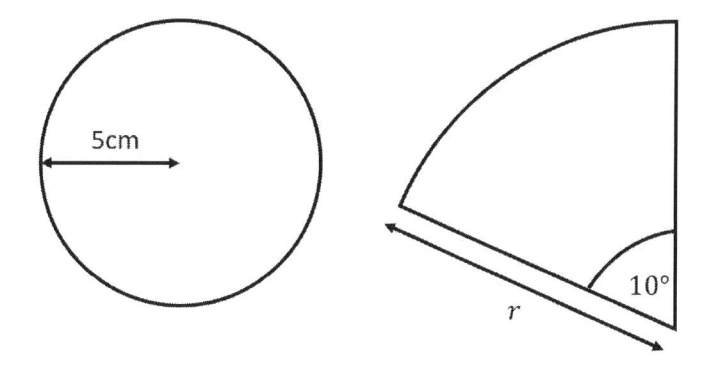

5cm

$10°$

r

Geometry

22

A circle is drawn inside a square.
The square is drawn inside a larger circle.
If the larger circle has an area of 36πcm², what is the area of the shaded region between the square and the smaller circle?
Give your answer to three significant figures.

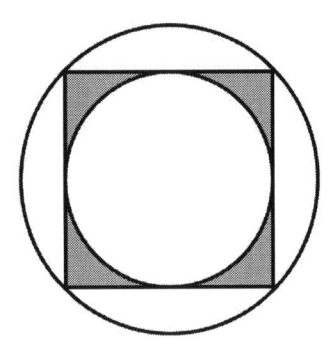

23

A cube of limestone is to be covered in a layer of marble to form a larger cube.
The marble will cover the limestone cube evenly to form the larger cube.
When the layer of marble is added the volume of the limestone cube increases by $\frac{61}{64}$.
The volume of the new larger cube is 1,000cm³.
What is the depth from the marble stone down to the limestone?

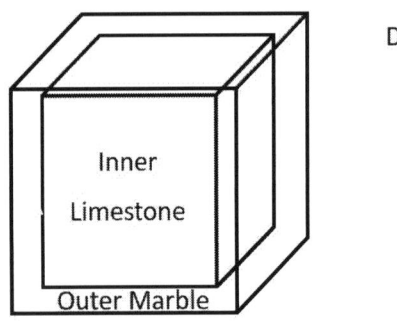

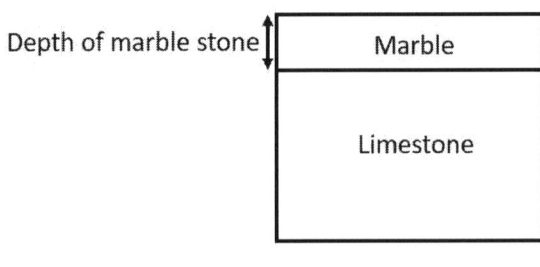

24

Three cylinders are stacked on top of each other in the diagram shown below.
The diagram is not to scale.
All the cylinders are similar.
Cylinder B has eight times the volume of cylinder A.
Cylinder C has eight times the volume of cylinder B.
Cylinder A has a height of 2cm.
What is the height, h of the entire stack?

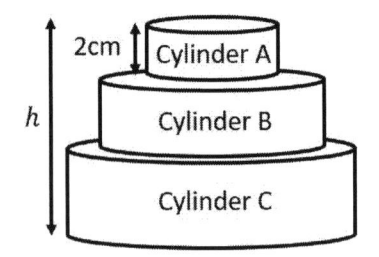

25

A new homeowner has recently moved into an area with two doctors surgeries nearby.
The homeowner wants to go to the nearest surgery.
The following information is available to the homeowner.
The New home is on a bearing of 040° from Surgery A.
Surgery A is x miles from the New home.
Surgery A and Surgery B are $1.6x$ miles apart.
Surgery B is on a bearing of 100° from Surgery A.
Which surgery is closer?

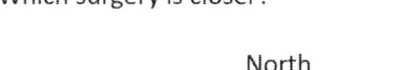

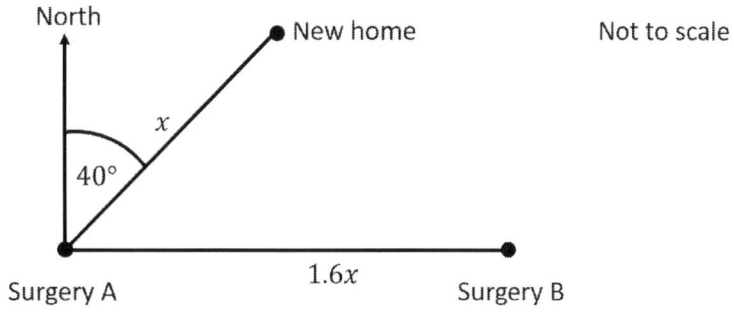

5 PROBABILITY

1

In a game, players must roll two dice and multiply the scores together shown on the dice.
To win a player must have a score that is a factor of 72.
A player rolls both dice.
What is the probability of winning?

2

A cyber security firm is looking to expand its number of employees.
Its sets a task to potential candidates to determine whether they have the necessary skills.
Candidates must break a code in under one hour.
If a candidate breaks the code in under one hour they are invited for an interview.
The probability of a candidate breaking the code in under one hour is 0.2.
Of those selected for interview, the probability of being offered a job is 0.3.
Find the probability that the first two candidates are both offered jobs at the cyber security firm.

3

A personal identification number (PIN) consists of four digits chosen from 0 to 9.
Each digit can be used more than once.
If the first and the third digits of the PIN are known, what is the probability of correctly guessing the PIN?

4

The probability that a stylus for a tablet PC will break in its first year is 0.1.
Find the probability that of three styluses purchased, exactly two will break in the first year.

5

The probability that a spider spins a web each day is 0.8 when the temperature is below or equal to 10°C.
The probability that a spider spins a web each day is 0.6 when the temperature is above 10°C.
If the spider spins a web, there is a probability of 0.7 of the spider catching a fly in the web.
In a study there are 1,400 days when the temperature is below or equal to 10°C and 1,050 days when the temperature is above 10°C.
Estimate what percentage of days in the study the spider caught a fly on.

GCSE Mathematics 9 – 1

6

The probability of rolling a 5 on a biased die is x.
The following probability ratio applies:
Rolling two 5's in a row : rolling two non 5's in a row = 9 : 4
Find the value of x.

7

There are an estimated three million words in the English language.
12% of the words are thought to be "slang" words.
The other words are "non-slang words".
What is the probability of selecting four words of which one is a slang word and three are non-slang words?
The words can be arranged in any order.
Give your answer to three significant figures.

6 ALGEBRA SOLUTIONS

1

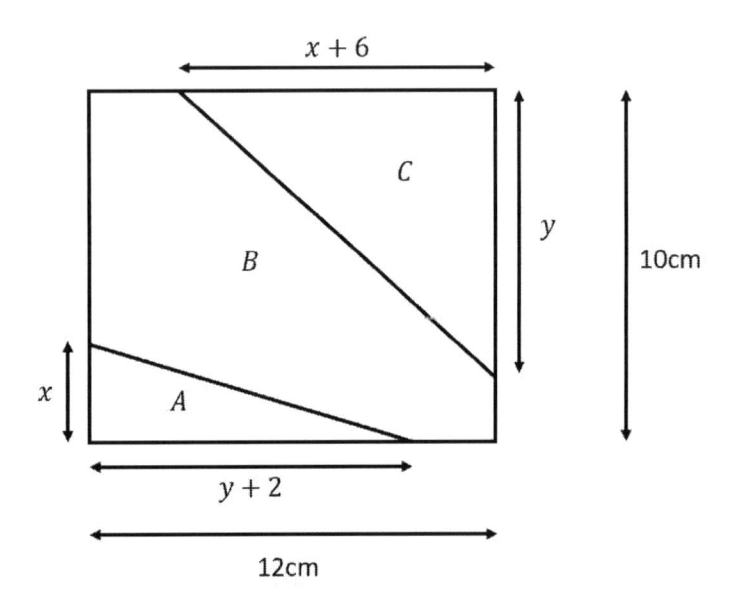

We need to find the area of the rectangle first:
$10 \times 12 = 120$
The area of the rectangle is 120cm².
We can now split this into the ratio $1 : 3 : 2$.
Since there are six parts here we can say that one part is equal to 20.
The area of triangle A is given by one part, so we can say:

$\frac{1}{2}bh = 20$ The area of a triangle is given by: $area = \frac{1}{2} \times base \times height$

$\frac{1}{2}x(y+2) = 20$

$x(y+2) = 40$ [1]   Multiply by 2 to form the first equation.

The area of triangle C is given by two parts, so we can say:

$\frac{1}{2}bh = 40$

$\frac{1}{2}y(x+6) = 40$

$y(x+6) = 80$ [2]   Multiply by 2 to form the second equation.

GCSE Mathematics 9 – 1

We now have two equations that we can solve using a substitution. If we rearrange equation [2] to make y the subject we obtain:

$$y = \frac{80}{x+6}$$ You have a pair of simultaneous equations to solve.

This can be substituted into equation [1] to give an equation in terms of x only:

$$x(y+2) = 40$$

$$x\left(\frac{80}{x+6} + 2\right) = 40$$

$$\frac{80x}{x+6} + 2x = 40 \qquad \text{Multiply out the brackets.}$$

$$80x + 2x(x+6) = 40(x+6) \qquad \text{Multiply by } (x+6).$$

$$80x + 2x^2 + 12x = 40x + 240 \qquad \text{Multiply out the brackets.}$$

$$2x^2 + 52x - 240 = 0 \qquad \text{Collect all the terms on one side.}$$

$$x^2 + 26x - 120 = 0 \qquad \text{Simplify the quadratic by dividing by 2.}$$

$$(x+30)(x-4) = 0 \qquad \text{Factorise the quadratic.}$$

$$x = -30, \quad x = 4$$

Only $x = 4$ is valid since x is a positive value.

We now substitute this value of x into the equation:

$$y = \frac{80}{x+6}$$
$$= \frac{80}{4+6}$$
$$= 8$$

The correct values are $x = 4$ and $y = 8$.

2

This is a law of indices based problem. Before we can form an equation to solve for x we need to make the bases the same for the equation given.

The bases are 4 and 8. These numbers are both powers of 2. This means we can write:

$$4 = 2^2, \qquad 8 = 2^3$$

These can be substituted into the original equation to give:

$$4^x = 8^{2x+2} \qquad \text{The law of indices:}$$

$$(2^2)^x = (2^3)^{2x+2} \qquad (a^m)^n = a^{mn}$$

$$2^{2x} = 2^{3(2x+2)}$$

$$2x = 3(2x+2) \qquad \text{Once the bases are the same we can say}$$

$$= 6x + 6 \qquad \text{that the powers are equal.}$$

$$-4x = 6 \qquad \text{Subtract } 6x.$$

$$x = -\frac{6}{4} \qquad \text{Divide by } -4.$$

$$= -\frac{3}{2}$$

Algebra Solutions

Now that we have solved for x we can evaluate 9^x.

$9^{-\frac{3}{2}} = \dfrac{1}{9^{\frac{3}{2}}}$

$= \dfrac{1}{\left(9^{\frac{1}{2}}\right)^3}$

$= \dfrac{1}{3^3}$

$= \dfrac{1}{27}$

The answer is $\dfrac{1}{27}$.

With a negative power (index) you write: "one over" the original term but with a positive power. For example:

$$5^{-2} = \dfrac{1}{5^2}, \quad 7^{-3} = \dfrac{1}{7^3}, \quad 8^{-\frac{2}{3}} = \dfrac{1}{8^{\frac{2}{3}}}$$

Split the fraction: $\dfrac{3}{2} = \dfrac{1}{2} \times 3$

The power $\dfrac{1}{2}$ means the square root so $9^{\frac{1}{2}} = 3$.

3

This is an identity as shown by the $\equiv$ symbol in the question.

Identities are not approached in the same way as solving an equation. With the identity we must find values of a, b and c that would make the coefficients of the x^2, x and constant terms the same for both sides. By coefficient, we mean the number in front of the letter. For $8x^2$, we would say that 8 is the coefficient of x^2. A constant refers to a lone number such as 10 or -34.

To find the values we start by expanding the brackets on the right-hand side of the identity:

$5x^2 - 40x + 8 \equiv ax^2 + 2(bx + c)^2$
$5x^2 - 40x + 8 \equiv ax^2 + 2(bx + c)(bx + c)$ Use F.O.I.L. when expanding two brackets:
$\equiv ax^2 + 2(b^2x^2 + bcx + bcx + c^2)$ First, Outer, Inner, Last.
$\equiv ax^2 + 2(b^2x^2 + 2bcx + c^2)$
$\equiv ax^2 + 2b^2x^2 + 4bcx + 2c^2$

We now start the process called "equating coefficients". This involves finding all the terms that contribute to the x^2 term, all the terms that contribute to the x term and all the terms that contribute to the constant on either side of the equation. From this we obtain:

$5x^2 - 40x + 8 \equiv (a + 2b^2)x^2 + 4bcx + 2c^2$ Note that x^2 has been factorised.

Now we can equate the coefficients to form a set of simultaneous equations:
$a + 2b^2 = 5$ [1]   For x^2 term.
$4bc = -40$ [2]   For x term.
$2c^2 = 8$ [3]   For the constant term.

The only equation we can begin to solve here is equation [3] because there is only one unknown letter, c, in the equation:
$2c^2 = 8$
   $c^2 = 4$ Divide by 2.
    $c = \pm 2$ Square root.

Remember that when you square root an answer there will be a positive and a negative answer.

We can now substitute these values for c into equation [2] to find b:
$4bc = -40$
  $bc = -10$ Divide by 4.
  $2b = -10$ Substitute $c = 2$.
   $b = -5$ Divide by 2.

Or,
  $bc = -10$
$-2b = -10$ Substitute $c = -2$.
   $b = 5$ Divide by -2.

These values for b can be substituted into equation [1].

Since the b term is squared in equation [1], it does not matter which value of b is chosen since both squares will give a positive value. Solving for a:
$a + 2b^2 = 5$
$a + 2(5)^2 = 5$
$a + 50 = 5$
$a = -45$
The answer is $a = -45$.

4

$2^x = 4^y$ [1]
$x^2 = 12y$ [2]
To solve these equations, we need to change the first equation so that the variables x and y are no longer in the powers.
Since 2 and 4 are both in the power series of 2 we can write:
$2^x = 4^y$
$\quad = (2^2)^y \qquad 4 = 2^2$
$\quad = 2^{2y}$
Since the base is now the same we can say that the powers must be equal:
$x = 2y$
We can substitute this into the second equation:
$\quad x^2 = 12y$
$(2y)^2 = 12y$
$\quad 4y^2 = 12y \qquad$ Divide by 4.
$\quad y^2 = 3y \qquad$ Do not just divide through by y here as you will lose one pair of the solutions.
$y^2 - 3y = 0 \qquad$ Instead move everything to the same side and set the quadratic equal to zero.
$y(y - 3) = 0 \qquad$ Factorise.
$y = 0$, or
$y - 3 = 0$
$\quad y = 3$
There are two solutions because we had a quadratic to solve. This means there will be two values of x:
When $y = 0$, $x = 0$ and when $y = 3$, $x = 6$ which are obtained from the equation $x = 2y$.

5

The area of a triangle can be found using the formula $area = \frac{1}{2}bh$ where b is the base and h is the height.
We need the base and the height of this triangle.
In general, it does not matter which you pick as long as the base and the height are perpendicular to each other.
We can select the distance from A to B for the base of the triangle and the x-coordinate of the intersection of the two lines will be the height of the triangle.
The distance from A to B is the difference between the y-intercepts of each line.
The intercepts are 2 and 26, which have a difference of 24; the base is 24 units.

Algebra Solutions

Now we find the x-coordinate by setting each of the lines equal to each other (we can do this because both equations are set equal to y).

$3x + 2 = -5x + 26$
$8x + 2 = 26$ Add $5x$.
$\quad 8x = 24$ Subtract 2.
$\quad\;\; x = 3$ Divide by 8.

The height of the triangle ABC is 3.
Now we can use the formula to find the area of triangle ABC:

$area = \dfrac{1}{2}bh$
$= \dfrac{1}{2} \times 24 \times 3$
$= 36$

The area of triangle ABC is 36 square units.

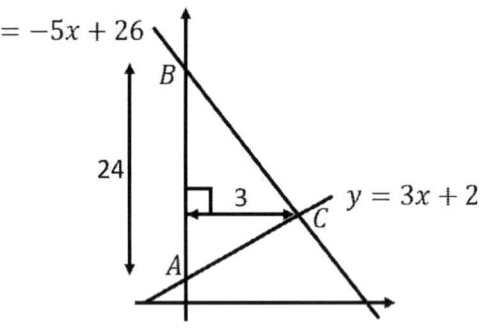

Both lines are in the form $y = mx + c$ where c is the y-intercept.

6

The motorbike will overtake the car at the instant when the car and the motorbike have travelled the same distance.
This means that we are looking for a time, which we will call T, at which this occurred.
On a velocity-time graph the area under the graph is the distance travelled.
We must write two expressions for the distance travelled by the car and the motorbike in terms of T.
Since both the car and the motorbike graphs form a triangle, this allows us to construct the expressions. This means we require a base and a height. The base will be given by the time axis but we can only get the height by using the equations of the lines that form the car and motorbike graph.
The equations are given as:
$V = 2.5t$ [1]
$V = 10t - 50$ [2]
These equations represent the vertical height of any triangle that we use.
For the car, the area of a triangle formed at time T will be given by:

$area = \dfrac{1}{2}bh$
$= \dfrac{1}{2} \times T \times 2.5T$ Substitute T in for t in the equation $V = 2.5t$.
$= \dfrac{1}{2} \times 2.5T^2$ Leave the area expression like this for now.

For the motorbike, the area of the triangle formed at time T will be given by:

$area = \dfrac{1}{2}bh$
$= \dfrac{1}{2} \times (T-5) \times (10T - 50)$
$= \dfrac{1}{2}(T-5)(10T-50)$

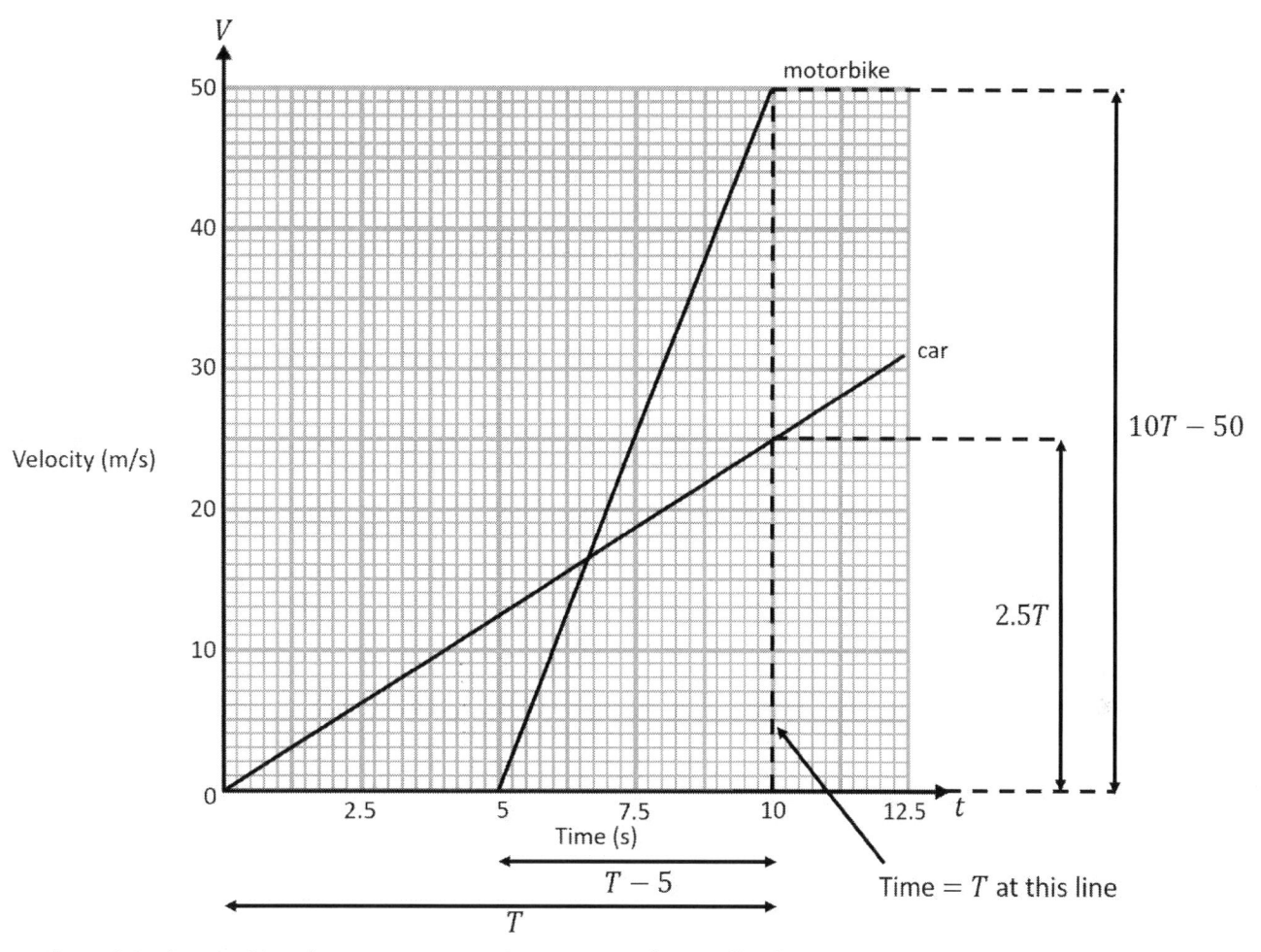

GCSE Mathematics 9 – 1

At the point of overtaking these area expressions are equal to each other:

$$\frac{1}{2} \times 2.5T^2 = \frac{1}{2}(T-5)(10T-50)$$

$$2.5T^2 = (T-5)(10T-50)$$ Multiply by 2.
$$= 10T^2 - 50T - 50T + 250$$ Expand the quadratic on the right hand side.
$$= 10T^2 - 100T + 250$$ Collect the terms onto one side so the quadratic is set equal to zero.
$$0 = 7.5T^2 - 100T + 250$$

Divide by 2.5 so the coefficients are integers.
$$3T^2 - 40T + 100 = 0$$ Factorise the quadratic.
$$(3T - 10)(T - 10) = 0$$

$$T = \frac{10}{3}, \quad T = 10$$

The value of T must be after five seconds since the motorbike did not start moving until then. The correct answer is $T = 10$.

The motorbike overtook the car 10 seconds after the car began to move.

Algebra Solutions

[Figure: Two right triangles. Left triangle labeled "motorbike" with vertical side $10T - 50$ and horizontal side $T - 5$. Right triangle labeled "car" with vertical side $2.5T$ and horizontal side T.]

These two triangles will have the same area when the motorbike overtakes the car.

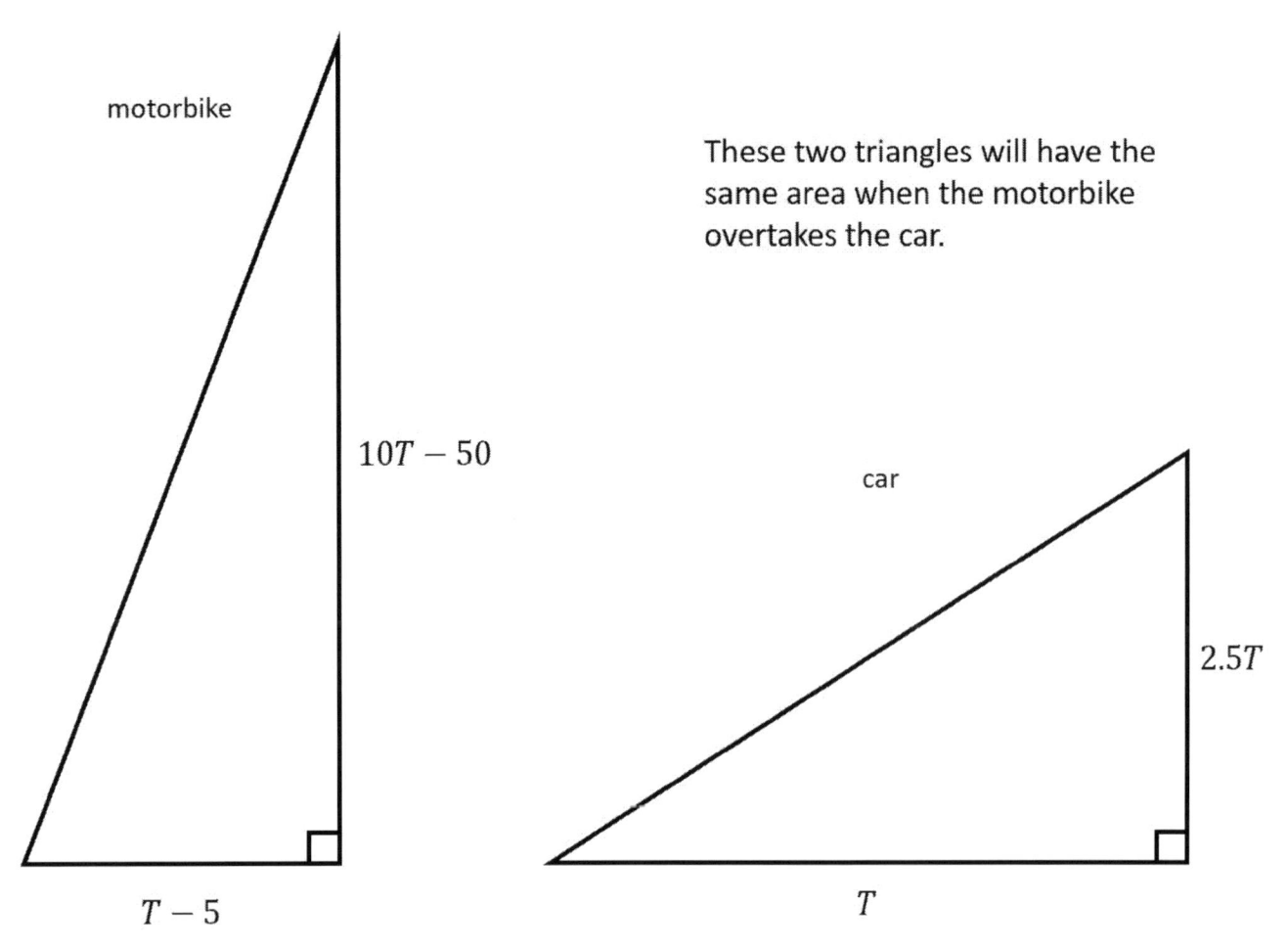

7

We have been given a generalised quadratic curve equation with unknown values a, b and c. We will use the facts about the trajectory of the golf ball to find these unknowns.

If the golf ball started at the origin then this is effectively a coordinate of (0,0). We can substitute $x = 0$ and $y = 0$ into the quadratic curve equation:

$y = ax^2 + bx + c$
$0 = a(0)^2 + b(0) + c$
$c = 0$

The next coordinate given that the golf ball travelled through was (80,64). This allows us to substitute these values into the quadratic curve equation:

$y = ax^2 + bx$
$64 = a(80)^2 + b(80)$
$64 = 6400a + 80b$
$\quad 4 = 400a + 5b \quad$ [2] $\qquad$ Divide by 16.

The next coordinate given that the golf ball travelled through was (150,15). This allows us to substitute these values into the quadratic curve equation:

$y = ax^2 + bx$
$15 = a(150)^2 + b(150)$
$15 = 22500a + 150b$
$\quad 1 = 1500a + 10b \quad$ [1] $\qquad$ Divide by 15.

We now have two simultaneous equations to solve.

GCSE Mathematics 9 – 1

We use the method of elimination to solve this pair of simultaneous equations.
We start by making the coefficient of b the same for both equations. This is achieved by multiplying the second equation by 2.

$1500a + 10b = 1$ [1] $\xrightarrow{\text{No change}}$ $1500a + 10b = 1$ [1]

$400a + 5b = 4$ [2] $\xrightarrow{\times 2}$ $800a + 10b = 8$ [3]

Subtract: [1] – [3]

$700a = -7$

$a = -\dfrac{1}{100}$

Substitute the value of a into equation [1].

$1500\left(-\dfrac{1}{100}\right) + 10b = 1$

$-15 + 10b = 1$ Add 15.

$10b = 16$ Divide by 10.

$b = 1.6$

$a = -\dfrac{1}{100}$ or -0.01
$b = 1.6$
$c = 0$

$y = -0.01x^2 + 1.6x$

8

Call the surface area percentage reduction A and the temperature T.
From the question we can state that $A \propto T^2$ (note that $\propto$ is the symbol of proportion).
We need to write a formula. To do this, we introduce the proportionality constant k.
So we write:
$A = kT^2$
To find k, we rearrange the formula to make k the subject and substitute a pair of values from the question for A and T. We know that $A = 8$ when $T = 40$:

$k = \dfrac{A}{T^2}$

$= \dfrac{8}{40^2}$

$= \dfrac{1}{200}$

So the formula is given by:

$A = \dfrac{T^2}{200}$

Algebra Solutions

The question states that the temperature is 40°C and then 30°C in the next two days.
We know that a day at 40°C reduces the area of the lake by 8 percent.
We will need to calculate the percentage reduction for 30°C:

$$A = \frac{30^2}{200}$$
$$= 4.5$$

So the area of the lake reduces by 4.5% when the temperature is 30°C.
There are three consecutive reductions in area of 8%, 8% and 4.5%.
The multipliers for these reductions are 0.92, 0.92 and 0.955.
Since the area of the lake at the start was 100km², we can multiply the values together to obtain the new area of the lake:
$100 \times 0.92 \times 0.92 \times 0.955 = 80.8312$
The area of the lake after the three days will be 80.8312km².

9

The volume of the cuboid is given by multiplying the length, width and depth together. We also know that this expression cannot exceed 175. From this we can write:

$$5x(x+2) \leq 175$$
$$x(x+2) \leq 35 \qquad \text{Divide by 5.}$$
$$x^2 + 2x \leq 35 \qquad \text{Multiply out the brackets.}$$
$$x^2 + 2x - 35 \leq 0 \qquad \text{Collect the terms to set the quadratic equal to zero.}$$
$$(x+7)(x-5) \leq 0 \qquad \text{Factorise.}$$

This is a quadratic inequality that will require a graphical interpretation to solve.
The quadratic will cross the x-axis at two different locations. These locations can be found by considering the equation $(x+7)(x-5) = 0$.
If we solve this equation we obtain two linear equations:
$x + 7 = 0, \qquad x - 5 = 0$
When each is solved we obtain $x = -7$ and $x = 5$.
These are the two points where the quadratic graph will cross the x-axis.
Since we are dealing with a positive quadratic, the shape of the graph will be a "bucket" (we call it a parabola but you do not need to call it that for now). See the graph and number line.

Now we look at the inequality $(x+7)(x-5) \leq 0$.
We are interested in where the quadratic graph is less than or equal to zero.
From a sketch of the graph we can see that this is when $-7 \leq x \leq 5$.
So we have our first range of values.
Now we will examine the second requirement and form another inequality.
The surface area of a cuboid is given by finding the area of three different faces and then multiplying by two.
We also know that this surface area must be greater than 76. From this we can write:

$$2 \times x(x+2) + 2 \times 5x + 2 \times 5(x+2) > 76$$
$$2x(x+2) + 10x + 10(x+2) > 76 \qquad \text{Multiply out the brackets.}$$
$$2x^2 + 4x + 10x + 10x + 20 > 76 \qquad \text{Collect the terms and set the quadratic equal to zero.}$$
$$2x^2 + 24x + 20 > 76$$
$$2x^2 + 24x - 56 > 0$$
$$x^2 + 12x - 28 > 0 \qquad \text{Divide by 2.}$$
$$(x+14)(x-2) > 0 \qquad \text{Factorise.}$$

GCSE Mathematics 9 – 1

This also forms a "bucket-shaped" quadratic graph. The locations of where this quadratic cuts the x-axis will be found by solving the two linear equations:
$x + 14 = 0, \quad x - 2 = 0$
Solving these we obtain $x = -14$ and $x = 2$.

There are two of each of the three faces shown below.

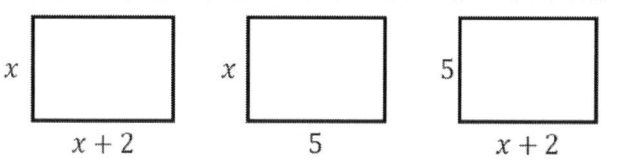

[Diagram: three rectangles labelled with sides x by $x+2$; x by 5; 5 by $x+2$.]

The inequality stated that we wanted to know where the graph was greater than zero. From the graph sketch we can see that this will be when either $x < -14$ or $x > 2$.

There are two things to note now. The first is that x must be positive since it is the actual length of a cuboid. The second is that we have two overlapping inequalities and we must select the region where both the inequalities overlap to find the correct range of values that x can take.

From the two graphs and the two inequality number lines, we can see that the values of x that overlap are given by $2 < x \leq 5$. This is the answer to the question.

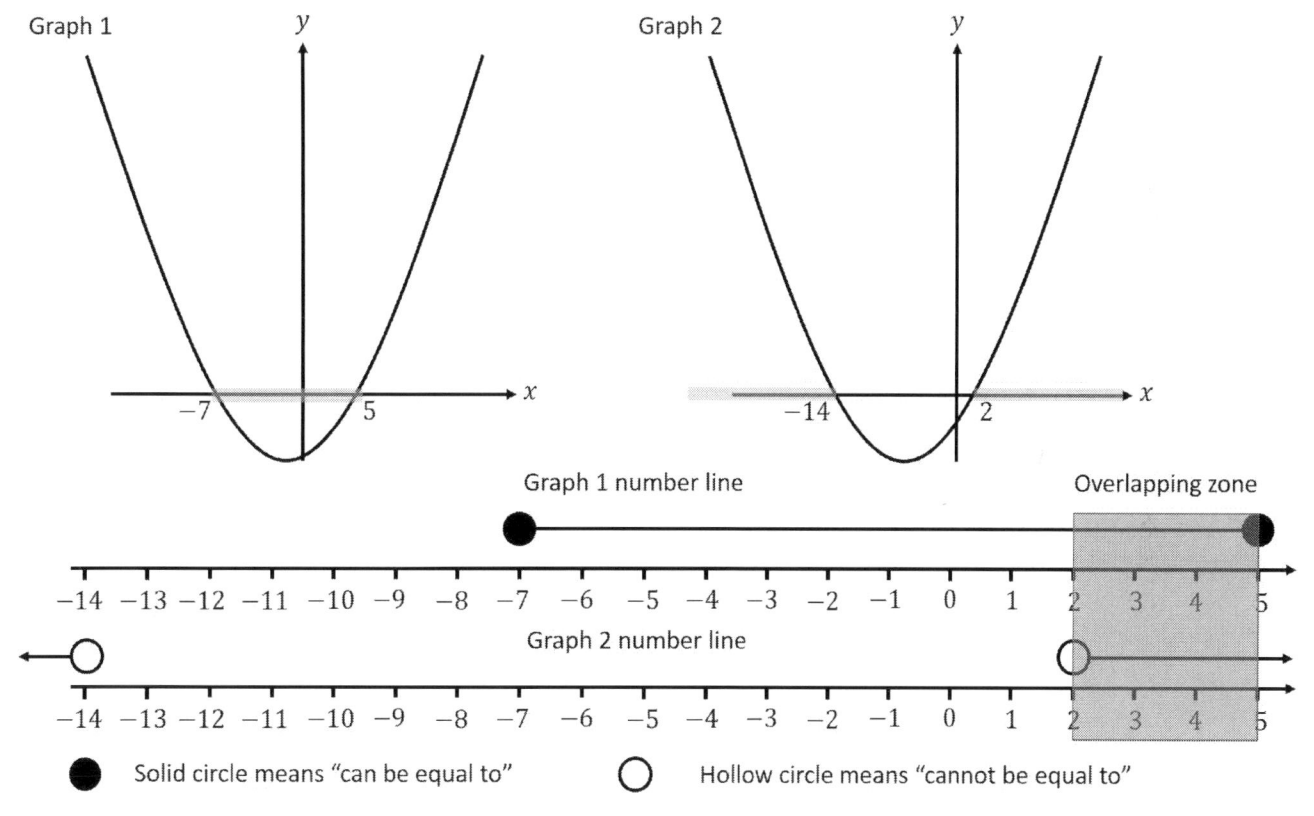

Graph 1: quadratic with roots at -7 and 5.

Graph 2: quadratic with roots at -14 and 2.

Graph 1 number line — solid circle, values to the right up to and including 5 (overlapping zone shaded from 2 to 5).

Graph 2 number line — hollow circle at -14 extending left; hollow circle at 2 extending right.

● Solid circle means "can be equal to"   ○ Hollow circle means "cannot be equal to"

10

This is a worded algebra problem.
If we let the son be x years old we can write expressions for all three family members in terms of x.
If the father is 250% the age of the son, then the father will be $2.5x$.
In four years' time the son will be $x + 4$ years and the grandfather will be three times as old as this.
We can say that the grandfather will be $3(x + 4)$ years old in four years' time.
At present the grandfather is 20 years older than the father.
We can say that the grandfather is $2.5x + 20$ years old now.

Algebra Solutions

Since we know the grandfather's age in four years' time, we can form an equation:
$3(x + 4) = 2.5x + 20 + 4$ Remember to add 4 to the grandfather's age now.
$3x + 12 = 2.5x + 24$ Multiply out the brackets and simplify.
$0.5x = 12$ Subtract $2.5x$ and subtract 12.
$x = 24$ Divide by 0.5.
The son is 24 years old.
The father will be $2.5 \times 24 = 60$ years old.
The grandfather is 80 years old.

11

We can start by finding the number of each type of customer.
10% of 800,000 is 80,000.
This means that 80,000 customers are contacted by post and 720,000 are contacted by email.
The total cost to contact 80,000 by post is $1.50 \times 80000 = 120000$.
Subtracting this value from £480,000 we obtain £360,000 which would have been spent on contacting customers by email.
Since there are 720,000 email customers, the amount spent per person would be:
$$\frac{360000}{720000} = 0.5$$
Therefore, 50p was spent per email customer.
$x = 50$.

12

This is a simultaneous equation problem. There are two variables to find: the rate at which the points are earned and the fixed amount of points your receive each time you spend. If there is more than one variable to find then you will need to form a set of simultaneous equations.
The question stated that the points were earned at a constant rate above a certain value. This is describing a linear relation: $y = mx + c$.
The value of m is the gradient, but it is also the rate at which the points are earned.
The value of c is the y-intercept, but it is also the amount of fixed points a customer is given.
The values of m and c are the variables that we need to find from a pair of simultaneous equations.
If a shopper spends £15 and accumulates 40 points then we can write:
$15m + c = 40$ [1]
If a shopper spends £25 and accumulates 60 points then we can write:
$25m + c = 60$ [2]
We now have a pair of linear simultaneous equations. We can solve them using the technique of elimination:
$15m + c = 40$ [1]
$25m + c = 60$ [2]
_____
$10m = 20$ Subtract: [2] − [1]
$m = 2$

Substitute $m = 2$ into [1]:
$30 + c = 40$
$c = 10$

Now that we have found the variables m and c we can substitute them into the original linear equation, $y = mx + c$ to get the required formula:
$y = 2x + 10$
This means you earn a fixed 10 points and then two points for every pound spent.

13

There are three separate requirements stated in the question which means that we will need to draw three inequality lines on the graph.
There is also no scale on the graph so we will let the y-axis go up to 250 and the x-axis go up to 250 since the number of cars or passengers will not exceed this amount.
Now we need to write the requirements as inequalities.
Since the number of cars is x, and it cannot be more than 100, we can say $x \leq 100$.
Since the number of passengers is y, and it cannot be more than 200, we can write $y \leq 200$.
The sum of cars and passengers must be at least 250 so we can write $x + y \geq 250$.
These inequalities can now be drawn on the graph.
Note that all the inequalities also allow the value to be "equal to". This means that we will draw solid lines on the graph instead of dashed lines.
When drawing inequalities, you can treat them in the same way as you would equations:
$x = 100, \qquad y = 200, \qquad x + y = 250$
These equations all describe lines. The last equation, $x + y = 250$, can be rewritten as:
$y = -x + 250$
This line has a gradient of -1 and a y-intercept of 250.
We require the area left of the line $x = 100$ since the number of cars must be no more than 100.
We require the area below the line $y = 200$ since the number of passengers must be no more than 200.
To find which side of $x + y \geq 250$ we require, try the origin $(0,0)$ in the inequality. If the origin with $x = 0$ and $y = 0$ satisfies the inequality, then we require the side with the origin in it. If it does not satisfy the inequality we require the side without the origin in it.

Substituting $x = 0$ and $y = 0$ into the inequality $x + y \geq 250$ we obtain:
$0 + 0 \geq 250$
This is not true so we require the side of the line without the origin.
The three lines are shown with the shaded region on the graph below:

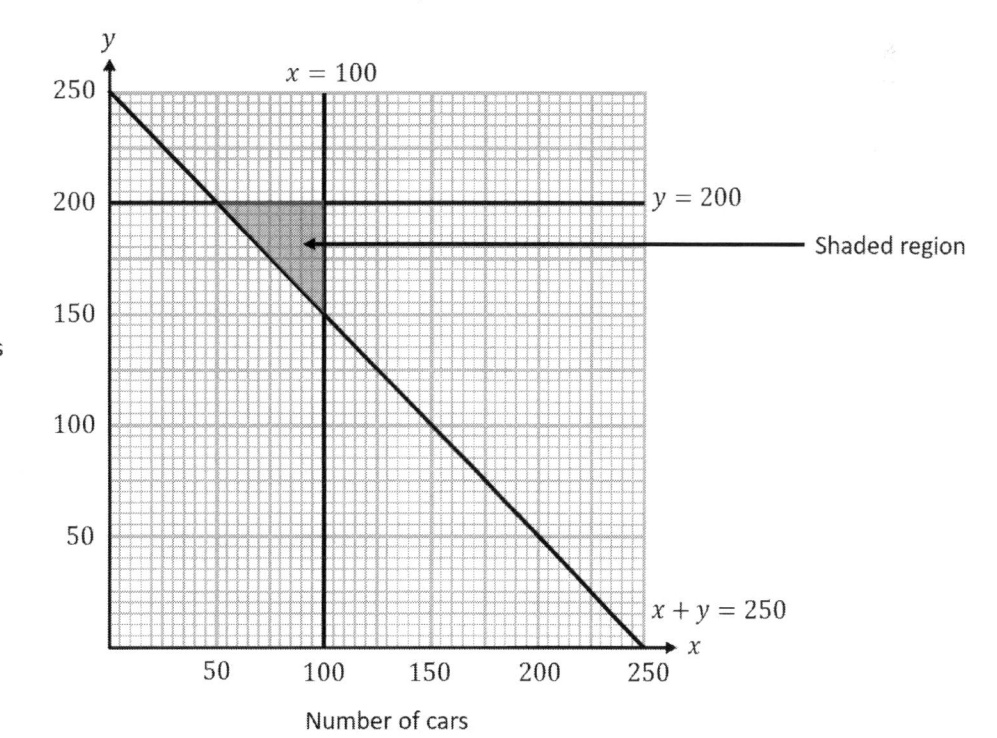

Algebra Solutions

14

If the input is x we can write an inequality that describes the given question:
The output of Machine A will be $x^2 + 2$.
The output of Machine B will be $(x - 3)^2$
Therefore:
four times the output of Machine A > three times the output of Machine B

$$4(x^2 + 2) > 3(x - 3)^2$$
$$4x^2 + 8 > 3(x - 3)(x - 3)$$
$$4x^2 + 8 > 3(x^2 - 3x - 3x + 9) \quad \text{Expand the brackets.}$$
$$4x^2 + 8 > 3(x^2 - 6x + 9)$$
$$4x^2 + 8 > 3x^2 - 18x + 27 \quad \text{Collect the terms of the quadratic on one side.}$$
$$x^2 + 18x - 19 > 0$$
$$(x + 19)(x - 1) > 0$$

We have formed a quadratic inequality. We need to find the locations of where this quadratic would cross the x-axis to determine the range of values that x can take. If we solve the equation:
$(x + 19)(x - 1) = 0$
$x + 19 = 0, \quad x - 1 = 0$
$x = -19, \quad x = 1$
We can now sketch a positive quadratic graph:

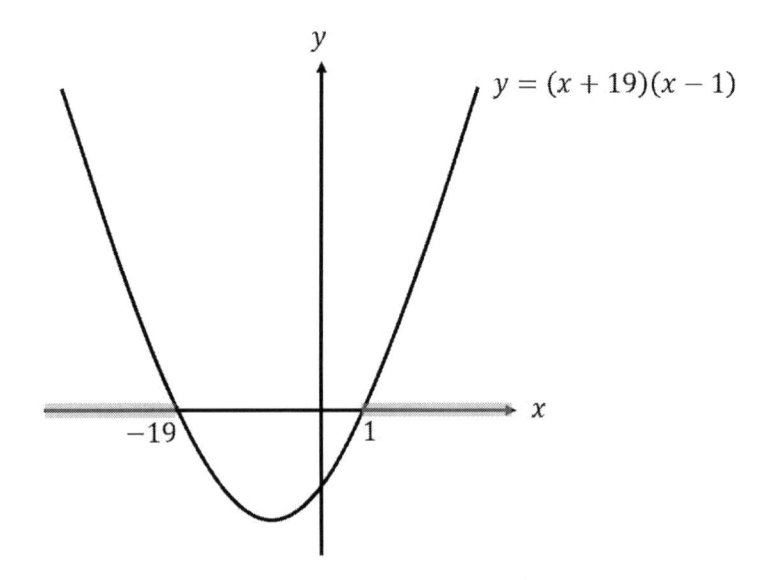

We need to select the region where the graph is above the x-axis.
There are two regions that satisfy the inequality, either $x < -19$ or $x > 1$.

15

The general equation of a positive quadratic is $y = (x + a)^2 + b$. From this equation we can determine the turning point of the quadratic as having the coordinates $(-a, b)$.
From the equation given we can see that $a = -3$ and $b = 0$.
This means the turning point for the graph of $y = (x - 3)^2$ will be $(3,0)$. Note that the sign of the "a" is changed and the sign of the "b" remains the same.
The turning point is at B from which we can say that B has coordinates $(3,0)$
To find an equation of a straight line you require the gradient and the y-intercept.
We can see from the graph that the line AC has a gradient perpendicular to the line AB and has a y-intercept which is the same as that of the curve $y = (x - 3)^2$.

The y-intercept is found by setting $x = 0$:
$$y = (x-3)^2$$
$$y = (0-3)^2$$
$$= 9$$
So the coordinates of A are $(0,9)$. This means that the line AC will have a y-intercept of 9.
We have the coordinates of A and B which allows us to calculate the gradient of AB. A gradient is found by dividing the difference in y by the difference in x.

$$gradient = \frac{9-0}{0-3}$$
$$= \frac{9}{-3}$$
$$= -3$$

The two coordinates are $(0,9)$ and $(3,0)$:   Difference in x ↕ ↕ Difference in y $(0,9)$ $(3,0)$

To find the gradient of AC we need to use the perpendicular gradient rule: take the reciprocal of the gradient and change the sign.

$$-3 \xrightarrow{\text{Reciprocal}} -\frac{1}{3} \xrightarrow{\text{Change the sign}} \frac{1}{3}$$

The gradient of AC is $\frac{1}{3}$. Since a straight line has the general equation $y = mx + c$ where m is the gradient and c the y-intercept, we write the equation of AC as $y = \frac{1}{3}x + 9$.

16

We need to examine the sequence to determine how each term is related.
The sequence is a power series of 3 with the next term found by multiplying the previous term by 3^2.
Since this is the same for all the terms we are dealing with a geometric sequence.
We now need to find a general expression for the nth term so we can calculate the difference between the 14th and 15th terms.
Notice that the powers of 3 for each term are the sequence of odd numbers: 1,3,5,7 ...
The odd numbers form a linear sequence of their own:

n	1	2	3	4
Sequence	1	3	5	7
1st difference		+2	+2	+2
$2n$	2	4	6	8
Residuals	−1	−1	−1	−1

Residuals:
$residuals = sequence - 2n$

The odd numbers have the general formula $2n - 1$.
This links to the powers of 3 so we can say that the general term is given by 3^{2n-1}.
Now that we have the general formula we can calculate the difference between the 14th and 15th term:
$$15th\ term - 14th\ term = 3^{2(15)-1} - 3^{2(14)-1}$$
$$= 3^{29} - 3^{27}$$
$$= 3^{27}(3^2 - 1) \qquad \text{Factorise } 3^{27} \text{ out.}$$
$$= 3^{27} \times 8$$

We do not need to calculate this value exactly, all we need to do is show that the difference is eight times the 14th term. The final line is $3^{27} \times 8$, but the 14th term is given by 3^{27}, and so we have proved that the difference between the 14th and 15th term is equal to eight times the 14th term.
In general for this sequence, the difference between successive terms will always be eight times the smaller of the two terms.

Algebra Solutions

17

The points on the graph do not appear to be linear as a line cannot be drawn that would connect all the points closely.
To get an idea of what the formula might be we need to look at the coordinates of some of the points.
We can see that the points (10,1) and (50,25) are plotted.

Cliff height (h metres)	Rate of retreat (R metres per year)
10	1
50	25

× 5 (for cliff height), × 25 (for rate of retreat)

If we examine how the two variables are related we can see that the cliff height has increased by a factor of 5 and the rate of retreat has increased by a factor of 25, which is the same as 5^2.
This suggests that the rate of retreat is proportional to the height of the cliff squared, $R \propto h^2$.
To find the formula we need to introduce the proportionality constant k.
This forms the equation $R = kh^2$.
To find k we substitute a pair of values (a coordinate pair) of R and h:
$R = kh^2$
$k = \dfrac{R}{h^2}$
$= \dfrac{1}{10^2}$
$= \dfrac{1}{100}$

This means the formula that connects R and h is $R = \dfrac{1}{100}h^2$.
To verify this you can try it out on the other four coordinates that we did not use:

Cliff height (h metres)	$R = \dfrac{1}{100}h^2$	Rate of retreat (R metres per year)
10	$\dfrac{1}{100} \times 10^2 = 1$	1
20	$\dfrac{1}{100} \times 20^2 = 4$	4
30	$\dfrac{1}{100} \times 30^2 = 9$	9
40	$\dfrac{1}{100} \times 40^2 = 16$	16
50	$\dfrac{1}{100} \times 50^2 = 25$	25

We can see that this formula is correct for all the coordinates plotted on the graph.

18

Call the amount that the millionaire has at the start x.
The millionaire has given away half his wealth at the time on five occasions.
The first amount given away will be $\dfrac{x}{2}$, then it will be $\dfrac{x}{4}$ since $\dfrac{1}{4}$ is half of $\dfrac{1}{2}$.

Continuing this sequence, we find that the total amount given away would be:
$$\frac{x}{2}+\frac{x}{4}+\frac{x}{8}+\frac{x}{16}+\frac{x}{32}=7750000 \quad \text{Five fractions for five years.}$$
If we write all these fractions over a common denominator we obtain:
$$\frac{16x}{32}+\frac{8x}{32}+\frac{4x}{32}+\frac{2x}{32}+\frac{x}{32}=7750000$$
$$\frac{31x}{32}=7750000$$
$$31x=248000000$$
$$x=8000000$$
The millionaire had a starting wealth of £8 million.

19

This is a speed-distance-time question. To form an equation to solve for x we note that the link in the question is that the total time of the journey was 5 hours. This means we can split the journey into two parts, one in congestion and the other not in congestion. From these parts we can write an expression for the time taken for the journey.

For the congestion part we can say:
$$time = \frac{distance}{speed}$$
$$= \frac{42}{x}$$

There will be $192 - 42 = 150$ miles left to travel with no congestion. For this part we can say:
$$time = \frac{distance}{speed}$$
$$= \frac{150}{50}$$
$$= 3$$

We know that the sum of these times must be 5, so we can write an equation:
$$\frac{42}{x}+3=5$$
$$\frac{42}{x}=2 \quad \text{Subtract 3.}$$
$$42=2x \quad \text{Multiply by } x.$$
$$x=21 \quad \text{Divide by 2.}$$
The mean speed when in congested traffic was 21mph.

20

We know that the quadratic goes through the origin which has coordinates (0,0). We can substitute these coordinates into the quadratic equation above to find c:
$$f(x)=x^2+bx+c \qquad f(x) \text{ can be treated as the ``}y\text{-coordinate''.}$$
$$0=0^2+b(0)+c$$
$$c=0$$

The quadratic is symmetric about $x = 2$. If the quadratic crosses the x-axis at the origin, it will also cross the x-axis at $x = 4$ since the origin and $x = 4$ are both two units away from the line $x = 2$. Therefore the other coordinate the quadratic passes through is (4,0). We can substitute these coordinates into the quadratic above to find b:

Algebra Solutions

$f(x) = x^2 + bx$
$0 = 4^2 + 4b$
$0 = 16 + 4b$
$4b = -16$
$b = -4$

The quadratic has the equation: $f(x) = x^2 - 4x$

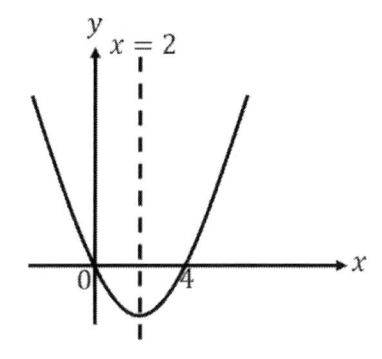

21

If 3,000 ebooks represented half the Total copies sold, then the Total copies sold will be:
$3000 \times 2 = 6000$
The Total copies sold is 6,000.
If 40% of year 11 students were sold paperbacks, then 60% were sold an ebook. This means we know that 60% of the year 11s was 3,000:
$60\% = 3000$
$1\% = 50$
$40\% = 2000$

2,000 year 11 students were sold a paperback.
The number of year 10 students will be: $6000 - 5000 = 1000$.
Equal numbers of year 10 students bought paperbacks and ebooks. From this we can calculate:
$\frac{1000}{2} = 500$
500 year 10 students were sold a paperback and 500 year 10 students were sold an ebook.
The total number of paperbacks will be given by:
$x = 2000 + 500$
$= 2500$
The completed frequency tree is shown below.

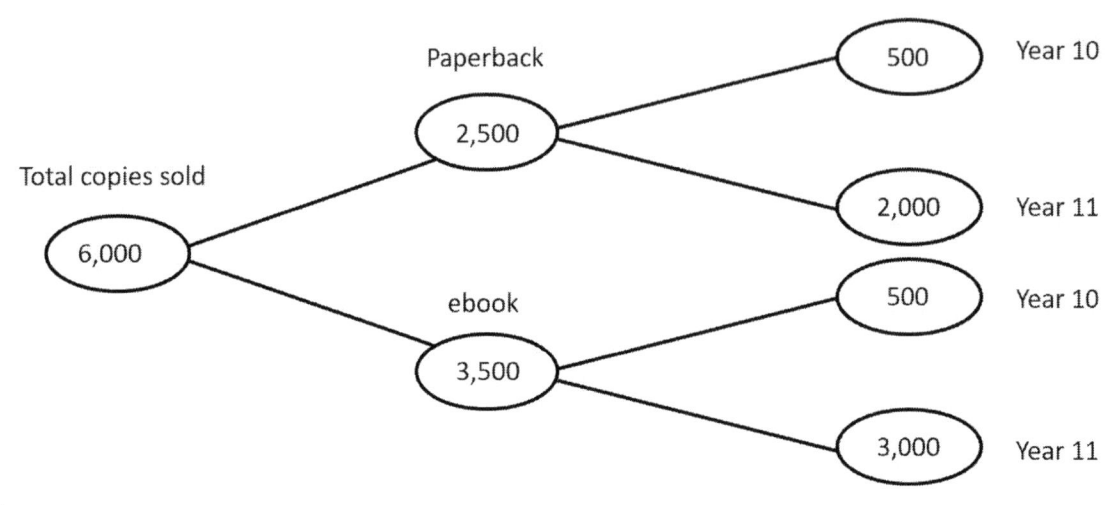

22

There are two formulae/relations to consider here.
The first is the formula involving force and pressure:
$pressure = \frac{force}{area}$
The second is the relation between the force and the volume of the object described in the first sentence:
$force \propto volume$

GCSE Mathematics 9 – 1

This question is based upon proportion so we do not need to know exact values, only comparisons (e.g. the large cylinder is twice as large).
If a cylinder has twice the height, its volume will be twice as great.
If a cylinder has twice the radius, its volume will be four times as great. This is because changing the radius changes the area of the circle in the cylinder. The area scale factor (ASF) is equal to the length scale factor (LSF) squared:
$ASF = LSF^2$
Since the length (radius) was doubled the LSF is 2, so the ASF will be 4. This means the circle will have four times the area and the resulting volume will be four times greater. If we combine this change with the height, the overall volume increase is eight times.
We have previously stated that the force is directly proportional to volume. This means that if the volume is eight times as great the force will be eight times as great.
One final consideration is that the second cylinder was stacked on top of the first cylinder. This means that the overall force exerted on the table will be nine times as great (the original cylinder and the larger cylinder combined).
Since the area in contact with the table has not changed (it is still the circular face of the smaller cylinder) the pressure will be nine times as great.

23

Start by multiplying through by the denominators:

$$5 + \frac{8(x+2)}{x+6} = 2.25(x+2)$$ Multiply through by $(x+2)$.
$$5(x+6) + 8(x+2) = 2.25(x+2)(x+6)$$ Multiply through by $(x+6)$.
$$5x + 30 + 8x + 16 = 2.25(x^2 + 6x + 2x + 12)$$ Expand the brackets.
$$13x + 46 = 2.25(x^2 + 8x + 12)$$ Collect the terms.
$$13x + 46 = \frac{9}{4}(x^2 + 8x + 12)$$ Change 2.25 into $\frac{9}{4}$.
$$52x + 184 = 9(x^2 + 8x + 12)$$ Multiply by 4.
$$52x + 184 = 9x^2 + 72x + 108$$ Expand the brackets.
$$0 = 9x^2 + 20x - 76$$ Collect the terms on one side and set the quadratic equal to zero.
$$0 = (9x + 38)(x - 2)$$ Factorise and solve.

$9x + 38 = 0$
$9x = -38$
$x = -\frac{38}{9}$
$x - 2 = 0$
$x = 2$

The solutions are $x = -\frac{38}{9}$ and $x = 2$.

24

The formula for the area of a trapezium is:
$$area = \frac{1}{2}h(a+b)$$
where h is the perpendicular distance between the parallel sides, a and b.
We will start by finding the area of the trapezium in Shape 1:
$$area = \frac{1}{2}(1)(2+4)$$
$$= 3$$
Now we will find the area of the second trapezium in Shape 2:
$$area = \frac{1}{2}(2)(2+6)$$
$$= 8$$

Algebra Solutions

Now we will find the area of the third trapezium in Shape 3:
$$area = \frac{1}{2}(3)(2+8)$$
$$= 15$$
Now we will find the area of the fourth trapezium in Shape 4:
$$area = \frac{1}{2}(4)(2+10)$$
$$= 24$$
Now we can put these results together in a table:

Shape number n	1		2		3		4
Area (cm²)	3		8		15		24
1st difference		+5		+7		+9	
2nd difference			+2		+2		
n^2	1		4		9		16
1st residuals	2		4		6		8
1st difference		+2		+2		+2	
$2n$	2		4		6		8
2nd residuals	0		0		0		0

Residuals:
$first\ residuals = area - n^2$

Remember to halve the second difference to find the coefficient of n^2.

Residuals:
$second\ residuals = first\ residuals - 2n$

From the table we can see that the area of the trapezia form a quadratic sequence with the nth term formula: $n^2 + 2n$.

25

The surface area of a cylinder is given by the two end circles and the rectangle formed between them. The rectangle will have a length equal to the height of the cylinder and a width equal to the circumference of the cylinder. The total surface area of the cylinder will be given by:
$area = two\ end\ circles + rectangle\ between$
$= 2\pi r^2 + 2\pi rh$
$= 2\pi r^2 + 2\pi r \times 10$
$= 2\pi r^2 + 20\pi r$

The question requires a range of values which will be given by an inequality:
$sphere\ surface\ area > cylinder\ surface\ area$

$$4\pi r^2 > 2\pi r^2 + 20\pi r \quad \text{Subtract } 2\pi r^2$$
$$2\pi r^2 > 20\pi r \quad \text{Divide by } 2\pi r$$
$$r > 10$$

The sphere has a larger surface area when the radius of each shape is greater than 10cm.

26

The surface area and the temperature are related proportionally by:
$$surface\ area \propto \frac{1}{temperature^2}$$
Call the surface area S and the temperature T.
We can then write:
$$S \propto \frac{1}{T^2}$$

This means that if the temperature is increased by a multiplier then the surface area will be divided by the square of that multiplier.

We require a ratio so we do not need to find a formula that connects surface area and temperature to answer this question. The way the surface area and temperature behave is best summarised in the table below:

Temperature (°C)	Surface area (cm²)
2	216
6	24

×3 ↓   ÷3²

In this question the temperature was changed from 2°C to 6°C, this is a multiplier of 3. This means that the surface area will be divided by 3^2 as the proportion requires:
$$\frac{216}{3^2} = 24$$
The surface area at 6°C is 24cm².
The ratio will be given by:
$surface\ area\ at\ 2°C : surface\ area\ at\ 6°C$
$$216 : 24$$
$$9 : 1$$

27

To find the fraction occupied by the circle we need the area of both the octagon and the circle.
The octagon is regular which means that it can be split into eight isosceles triangles that all have one side of 10cm. The equal angles will be found by splitting an interior angle in half. The circle can also be split into eight sectors with the radius equal to the height of the isosceles triangle. The sector will occupy the same fraction of the isosceles triangle as the whole circle does of the entire octagon.
Each interior angle of a regular octagon will be the same. We can use the interior angle formula to find the size of these angles for a polygon of n sides:
$$interior\ angle = \frac{180(n-2)}{n}$$
$$= \frac{180(8-2)}{8} \quad n = 8 \text{ for an octagon.}$$
$$= 135°$$
Halving this angle we obtain 67.5°.
We can also calculate the remaining angle as 45°, see the diagram.

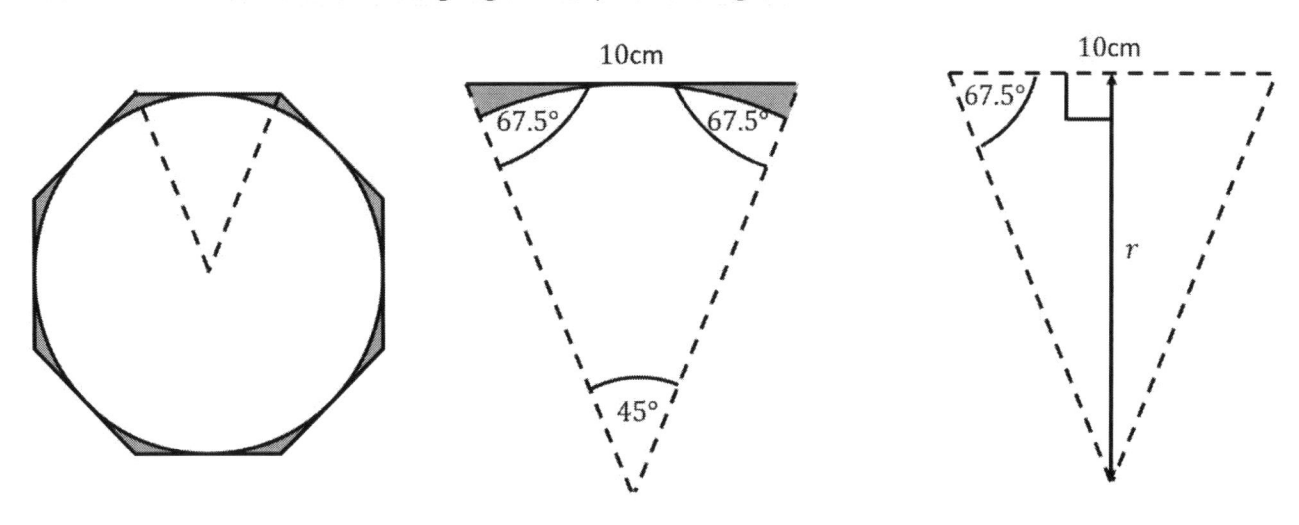

Algebra Solutions

We now need the area of the sector and the area of the triangle. The area of the sector can be found using the following formula:

$$\text{area of sector} = \frac{\text{angle of sector}}{360} \times \pi r^2$$
$$= \frac{45}{360} \times \pi r^2$$
$$= \frac{\pi r^2}{8}$$

The area of the triangle can be found by finding the height of the isosceles triangle by splitting the triangle in half. The height of the triangle formed will be the same as the radius of the circle, r.

The area of the triangle is given by:

$$\text{area} = \frac{1}{2} \times \text{base} \times \text{height}$$
$$= \frac{1}{2} \times 10 \times r$$
$$= 5r$$

Now we can find the fraction of the triangle occupied by the sector by simplifying the following:

$$\text{fraction occupied} = \frac{\text{area of sector}}{\text{area of triangle}}$$
$$= \frac{\frac{\pi r^2}{8}}{5r}$$
$$= \frac{\pi r^2}{8} \div 5r$$
$$= \frac{\pi r^2}{8} \times \frac{1}{5r}$$
$$= \frac{\pi r^2}{40r}$$
$$= \frac{\pi r}{40}$$

For fraction division:
Multiply by the reciprocal of the second fraction, so that $5r$ becomes $\frac{1}{5r}$.
Cancel r from both numerator and denominator.

We previously stated that this fraction would be the same as the fraction occupied by the circle of the whole octagon so we have correctly shown the required fraction.

28

We can write the proportion given in the question as:
$l \propto \sqrt{h}$
We turn this into an equation with the introduction of a proportionality constant k:
$l = k\sqrt{h}$
To find k we need to rearrange the equation to make k the subject and substitute a pair of values for l and h. We have a pair of values given in the question, $l = 70$ and $h = 196$.

$$k = \frac{l}{\sqrt{h}}$$
$$= \frac{70}{\sqrt{196}}$$
$$= 5$$

So the formula is $l = 5\sqrt{h}$.

When the height of the radio mast is 256m we require:
$l = 5\sqrt{256}$
$= 80$

GCSE Mathematics 9 – 1

We need 80m of wire for a 256m radio mast.
The extra wire required is given by $80 - 70 = 10$m.
An extra 10m of wire are required.
The table shows how the multipliers work for this type of proportion.

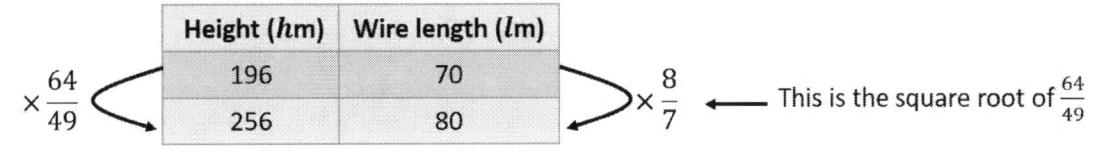

Height (hm)	Wire length (lm)
196	70
256	80

$\times \dfrac{64}{49}$ (left side), $\times \dfrac{8}{7}$ (right side) ← This is the square root of $\dfrac{64}{49}$

29

The question is describing two inequalities that we must form and solve to find the range of values that n can be. The formula for the exterior angle of a regular polygon of n sides is:
$$exterior\ angle = \frac{360}{n}$$
This means that we can form an inequality:
$\dfrac{360}{n} < 10$
$360 < 10n$ Multiply by n.
$36 < n$ Divide by 10.

The formula for the interior angle of a regular polygon of n sides is:
$$interior\ angle = \frac{180(n-2)}{n}$$
This means that we can form an inequality:
$\dfrac{180(n-2)}{n} < 175$
$180(n-2) < 175n$ Multiply by n.
$180n - 360 < 175n$ Multiply out the brackets.
$\quad 5n < 360$ Add 360 and subtract $175n$.
$\quad n < 72$ Divide by 5.

These two inequalities combine to give $36 < n < 72$.

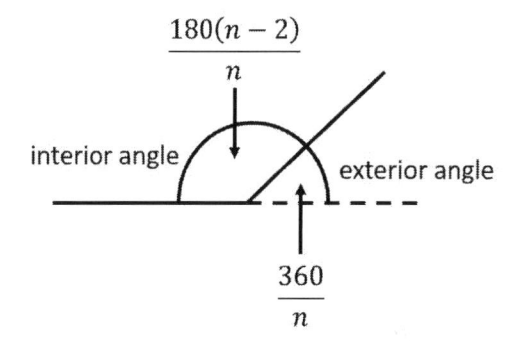

30

The object decreases by $x\%$ for every 500m. During the last 2,000m this percentage reduction will be applied four times since $\dfrac{2000}{500} = 4$.

To convert $x\%$ to a decimal we divide by 100 to give:
$$\frac{x}{100}$$
This is also a percentage reduction so we will need to subtract the decimal $\dfrac{x}{100}$ from 1 to give:
$$1 - \frac{x}{100}$$
This is the overall multiplier used to give an $x\%$ reduction.
Since this reduction is applied four times we need to introduce a power:
$$\left(1 - \frac{x}{100}\right)^4$$
This multiplier will be applied to the initial velocity V to obtain the final velocity on landing S:
$$S = V \times \left(1 - \frac{x}{100}\right)^4$$
$$= V\left(1 - \frac{x}{100}\right)^4$$

Algebra Solutions

31

This is a simultaneous equation question.
Call Student A's number x.
Call Student B's number y.

From what the Student A said:
$x^2 + 5 = y^2 - 6$
$\quad x^2 = y^2 - 11 \quad [1]$ Subtract 5.

From what Student B said:
$x + y = 11$
$\quad y = 11 - x \quad [2]$ Subtract x.

Substitute [2] in [1]:
$x^2 = y^2 - 11$
$\quad = (11 - x)^2 - 11$
$\quad = (11 - x)(11 - x) - 11$ Expand the brackets.
$\quad = 121 - 11x - 11x + x^2 - 11$ Collect the terms.
$\quad = 110 - 22x + x^2$
$0 = 110 - 22x$ Subtract x^2.
$22x = 110$ Add $22x$.
$x = 5$ Divide by 22.
$y = 6$ Substitute $x = 5$ into equation [2] to obtain y.

Student A: 5
Student B: 6

32

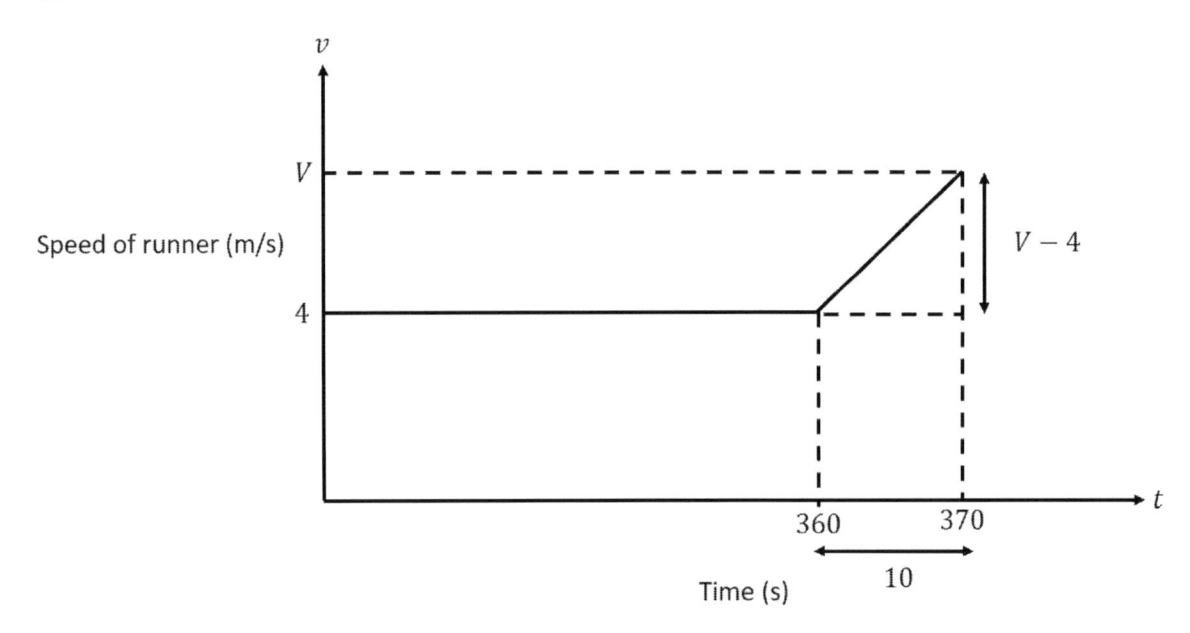

We can start by sketching a graph to give a better idea of how the speed of the runner varied for the race:
Since this is a speed-time graph we know that the area under the graph will be the total distance travelled (which was given as 1,500m).

The area is formed from a triangle and a rectangle. The final velocity we can call V. This means that we can write an equation for the area under the graph:

$$rectangle + triangle = area$$
$$lw + \frac{1}{2}bh = 1500$$

$370 \times 4 + \frac{1}{2} \times 10 \times (V-4) = 1500$ Substitute the correct values into the area formulae.

$1480 + 5(V-4) = 1500$ Simplify.

$1480 + 5V - 20 = 1500$ Multiply out the brackets.

$5V + 1460 = 1500$

$5V = 40$ Subtract 1460.

$V = 8$ Divide by 5.

The final speed of the runner is 8m/s.

33

This is a worded algebra problem.
We can convert the statements in the question into equations.
Call the interquartile range of Box Plot B x; the interquartile range of Box Plot A will be $x + 11$.
Call the range of Box Plot B y; the range of Box Plot A will be $y + 32$.
From the next two points we can form an equation involving x and y:

$20 + 21 + x + 11 = y + 32$

$x + 52 = y + 32$ Collect terms.

$x + 20 = y$ [1]   Subtract 32.

From the final point we can form another equation involving x and y:

$y = 3.5x$ [2]

We can equate [1] and [2]:

$3.5x = x + 20$

$2.5x = 20$ Subtract x.

$x = 8$ Divide by 2.5

$y = 8 + 20$

$y = 28$

Since y represented the range of Box Plot B the answer is 28.

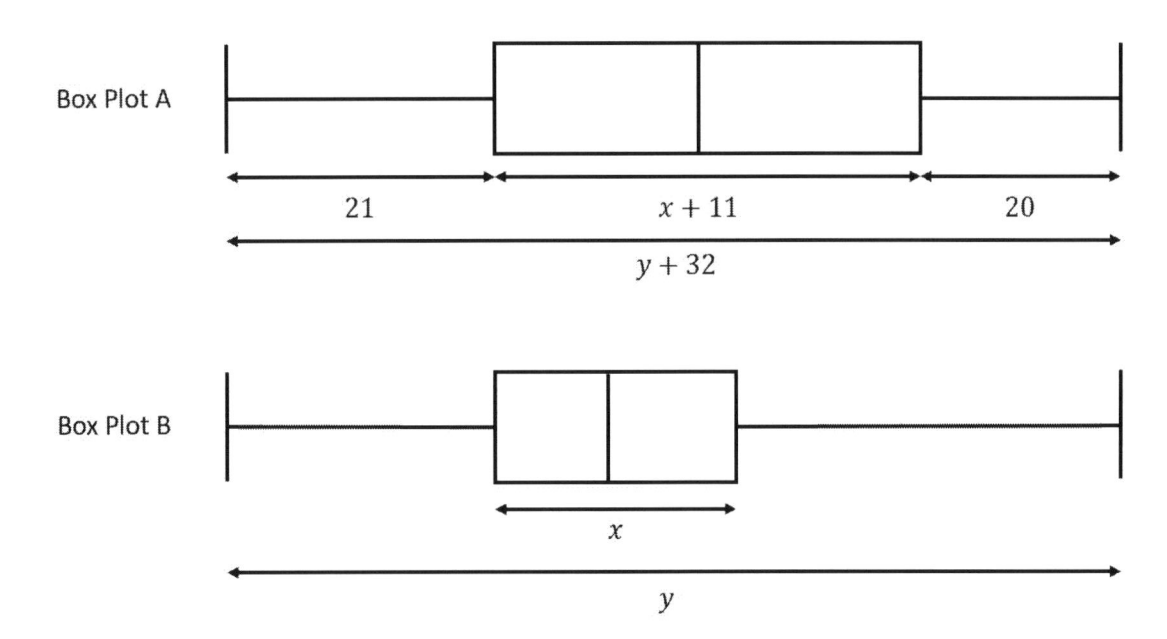

Algebra Solutions

34

This is a worded algebra question. We can call the not satisfied "pay as you go" number x.
If five times as many people on contract were not satisfied as the people not satisfied on pay as you, then we can call the not satisfied contract number $5x$.
If $\frac{9}{10}$ on "pay as you go" were satisfied then we can represent this number by $9x$, since this would be nine times the number on "pay as you go" who were not satisfied.
If $\frac{3}{4}$ of the people were on contract, then $\frac{1}{4}$ were on "pay as you go". Since we have a total of $10x$ on "pay as you go" we can say that $30x$ must be on contract. This is because $\frac{3}{4}$ is three times $\frac{1}{4}$.
If 252 more people were satisfied than not satisfied, we can form an equation in x to solve.
All parts of the frequency tree can be completed in terms of x as shown in the diagram.

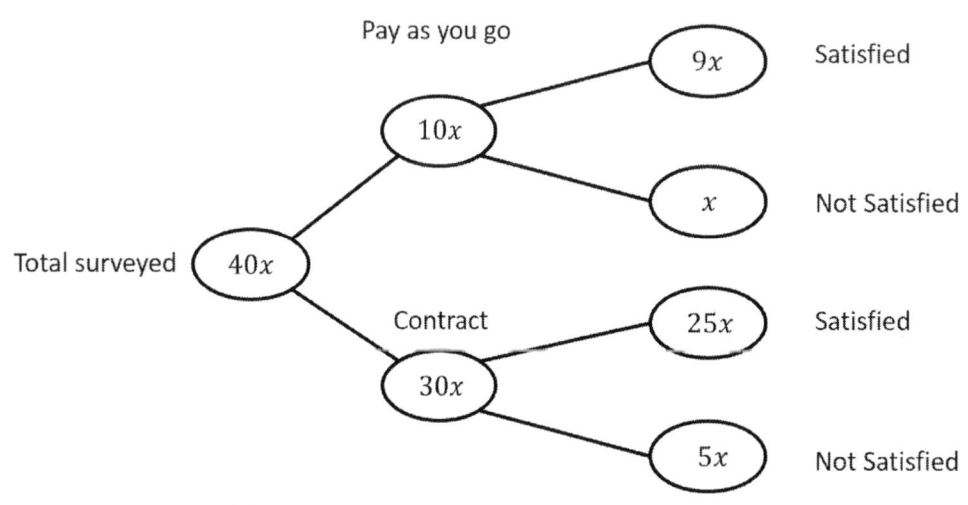

Frequency tree:
- Total surveyed: $40x$
  - Pay as you go: $10x$
    - Satisfied: $9x$
    - Not Satisfied: x
  - Contract: $30x$
    - Satisfied: $25x$
    - Not Satisfied: $5x$

The equation required will be:
$25x + 9x = 5x + x + 252$
$34x = 6x + 252$ Collect the terms.
$28x = 252$ Subtract $6x$.
$x = 9$ Divide by 28.

From this we can complete the frequency tree as shown below.

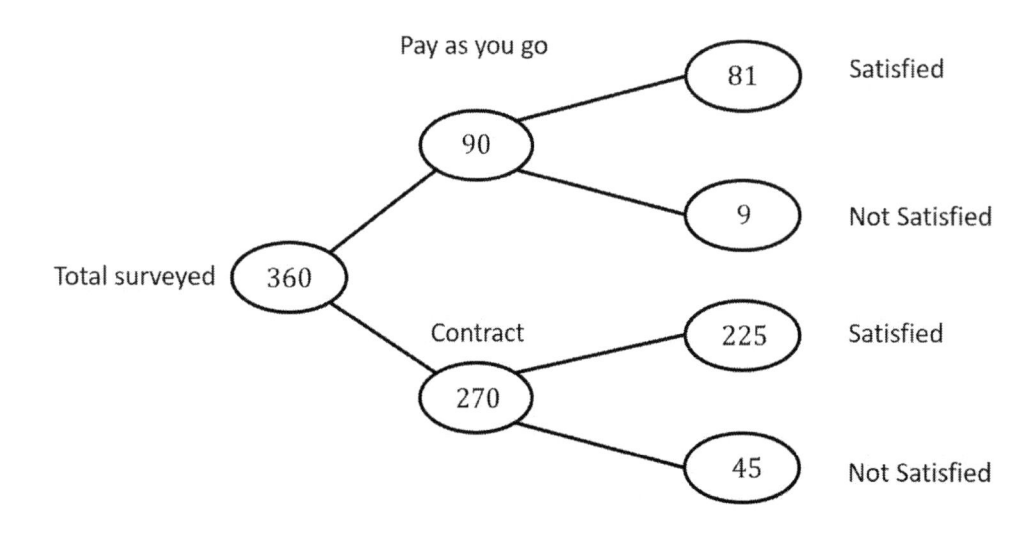

Frequency tree:
- Total surveyed: 360
  - Pay as you go: 90
    - Satisfied: 81
    - Not Satisfied: 9
  - Contract: 270
    - Satisfied: 225
    - Not Satisfied: 45

7 RATIO SOLUTIONS

1

There are two circle theorems required to answer this question, they are:
- Angles in the same segment
- Alternate segment theorem

The first theorem to use is the "angles in the same segment". We can say that $y = 70°$ because that angle is in the same segment as angle BEF.

If angle $BEF = 70°$ then angle $ABF = 70°$ by the alternate segment theorem.

If angle $ABF = 70°$ then angle $ABC = 48°$ since $70° - 22° = 48°$.

We know that angle $ACB = 90°$ because ACG is a straight line (tangent).

This means that x can be calculated:

$x = 180° - 90° - 48°$
$ = 42°$

Now we can find the ratio of $y : x$.

$y : x$
$70° : 42°$
$5 : 3$

The correct answer is $5 : 3$

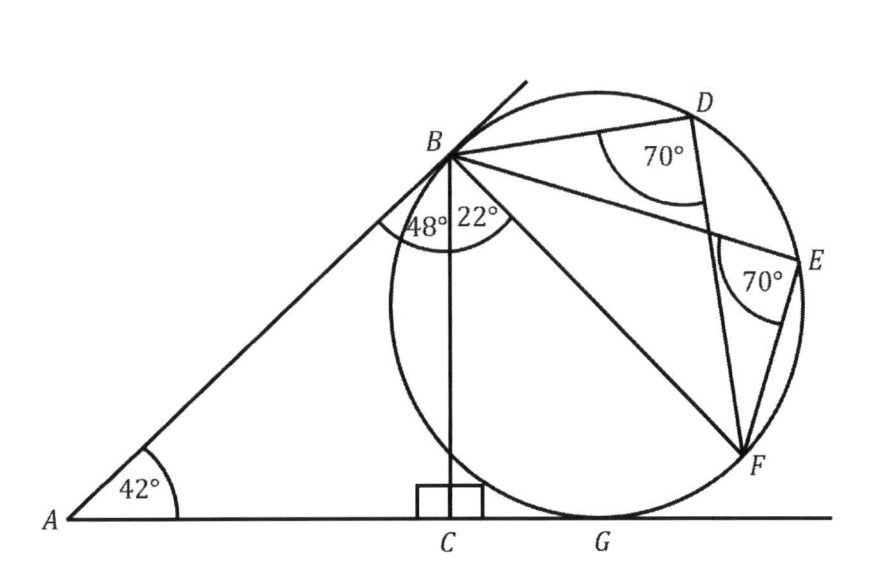

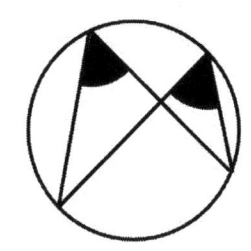

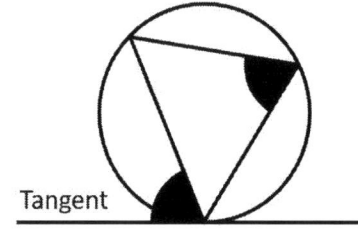

Ratio Solutions

2

The area of a parallelogram is given by the base multiplied by the vertical height. In the case of the question, it will be $l \times h$.
We are given two separate ratios that are connected by w. We can use the ratio $w : h$ to find w given that we know $h = 20\sqrt{3}$cm.

$w : h$
$2 : \sqrt{3}$
$40 : 20\sqrt{3}$
$w = 40$

Now we can use the ratio connecting l and w.
$l : w$
$3 : 2$
$60 : 40$
$l = 60$

We can now calculate the area of the parallelogram.
$area = lh$
$= 60 \times 20\sqrt{3}$
$= 1200\sqrt{3}$

The area of the parallelogram is $1200\sqrt{3}$cm².

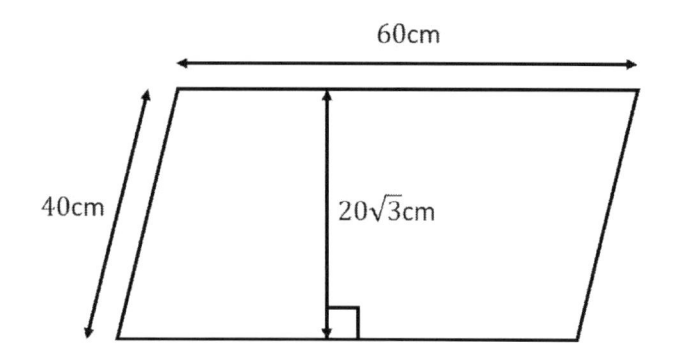

3

The general formula for the volume of a cylinder is given by:
$volume = \pi r^2 h$
The general formula for the volume of a hemisphere is given by:
$volume = \frac{2}{3}\pi r^3$ A hemisphere is half a sphere hence half the volume.
The hemisphere is half the sphere.
The volumes of each of these solids are equal. This allows us to find a simplified relation between r and h from which we can write a ratio.
$volume\ of\ hemisphere = volume\ of\ cylinder$
$\frac{2}{3}\pi r^3 = \pi r^2 h$
$\frac{2}{3}r = h$ Divide by πr^2.
$2r = 3h$ Multiply by 3.

We can now form the ratio by switching the numbers between the terms:
$r : h$
$3 : 2$
The correct answer is $3 : 2$

4

We will begin by calculating volumes that are given in the question. We are told that 600cm³ of Mixture A are poured into the tank in the ratio 5:1.
This means that we can split this ratio:
$6\ parts = 600$
$1\ part = 100$
So the water added so far will be 500cm³ and the syrup added 100cm³.
We do not know the exact volume of Mixture B that was added but we do know that Mixture B is in the ratio 8:1.

GCSE Mathematics 9 – 1

We can rewrite this ratio as $8x : x$ where x is a constant to be determined. The true volume of water and syrup added by Mixture B is represented by $8x : x$.
We can now combine this volume with that of Mixture A:
$$water : syrup$$
$$8x + 500 : x + 100$$
This ratio represents the true volumes of water and syrup in the tank.
We also know what the final ratio was in the tank, 6:1.
We can now link the ratio 6:1 with the algebra ratio $8x + 500 : x + 100$.

We do this by cross multiplying the values in the ratios to give:

$1 \times (8x + 500) = 6 \times (x + 100)$	
$8x + 500 = 6x + 600$	Subtract $6x$.
$2x + 500 = 600$	Subtract 500.
$2x = 100$	Divide by 2.
$x = 50$	

$$8x + 500 : x + 100$$
$$6 : 1$$

The volume V of Mixture B added was given by the ratio $8x : x$.
Since we know that $x = 50$ we can substitute this into the ratio to find V:
$8x : x$
$400 : 50$
450cm³ of Mixture B was added to the tank.

5

Let the original speed of the bird be V_{bird} and the original speed of the insect be V_{insect}.
This is a percentage multiplier problem. The multiplier for a 10% decrease is 0.9 and the multiplier for a 70% decrease is 0.3.
From the statement in the question we can form an equation:

$V_{bird} \times 0.9^3 = V_{insect} \times 0.3^3$ The power of 3 is used because the decrease was applied three times.
$0.729 V_{bird} = 0.027 V_{insect}$
$\dfrac{0.729 V_{bird}}{0.027} = V_{insect}$ Divide by 0.027.
$27 V_{bird} = V_{insect}$ Integers are easier to deal with than decimals when converting to a ratio.

We can now write the ratio as:
$V_{bird} : V_{insect}$ We can turn the equation into a ratio by swapping the constants 27 and 1:
$1 : 27$
The correct answer is 1 : 27

$$27 V_{bird} = V_{insect}$$
$$1 : 27$$
$$V_{bird} : V_{insect}$$

6

The ratio tells us that the height is ten times the radius: $h = 10r$
Since we know the volume of the cone we can set this equal to the formula, substitute the value of h for $10r$ and then solve for r.

$\dfrac{1}{3}\pi r^2 h = 720\pi$	Divide by π and substitute $h = 10r$.
$\dfrac{1}{3} r^2 (10r) = 720$	
$10r^3 = 2160$	Multiply by 3.
$r^3 = 216$	Divide by 10.
$r = 6$	Cube root.

Ratio Solutions

The radius of the cone is 6cm. the height of the cone will be:
$h = 10r$
$ = 10 \times 6$
$ = 60$

You could have also substituted $r = \frac{h}{10}$ and solved for h, both give the same answer of $h = 60$.

The height of the cone is 60cm.

7

A set of ordered data can be used to form a box plot of the general shape shown in the diagram below:

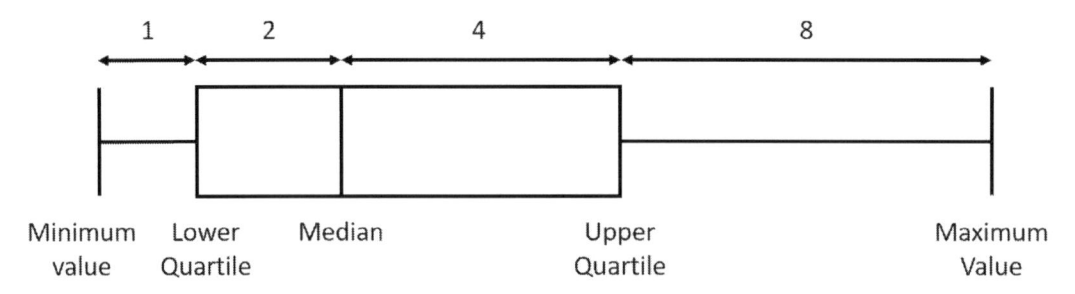

[Box plot diagram with segments labeled 1, 2, 4, 8 between Minimum value, Lower Quartile, Median, Upper Quartile, and Maximum Value]

The question is based upon ratios of the distances between the points on the box plot.
Being a ratio question, we do not need exact values, only relative sizes.
If we call the distance between the minimum value and the lower quartile "1", then we can call the distance between the lower quartile and median "2".
Since the distance between the median and upper quartile is twice that of the distance between the lower quartile and median, we can call this distance "4".
The distance between the maximum value and the upper quartile is twice the distance between the upper quartile and the median so we can call this distance "8".
The range will have a value of $1 + 2 + 4 + 8 = 15$.
The interquartile range will have a value of $2 + 4 = 6$.
The ratio of range to interquartile range will be given by:
$range : interquartile\ range$
$15 : 6$
$5 : 2$

The correct answer is $5 : 2$

8

If the cylinder takes four times as long as the cone to fill then the cylinder must have a volume that is four times larger than that of the cone. From this we can write the equation:
$volume\ of\ cylinder = 4 \times volume\ of\ cone$
$\pi r^2 h_{cylinder} = 4 \times \frac{1}{3}\pi r^2 h_{cone}$
$h_{cylinder} = \frac{4}{3} h_{cone}$ Divide by πr^2
$3h_{cylinder} = 4h_{cone}$ Multiply by 3

$h_{cylinder}$ is the height of the cylinder.
h_{cone} is the height of the cone.

From this result we can obtain the ratio:
$height\ of\ cylinder : height\ of\ cone$
$4 : 3$

We can turn the equation into a ratio by swapping the constants 3 and 4:
$3h_{cylinder} = 4h_{cone}$
$\phantom{3h_{cyli}}4 : 3$
$height\ of\ cylinder : height\ of\ cone$

The correct answer is $4 : 3$

9

All three solids have the same density. If we examine the formula that connects density, mass and volume:
$$density = \frac{mass}{volume}$$
$$density \times volume = mass$$
$$volume = \frac{mass}{density}$$

We can see that the mass is on the numerator of this fraction. This means that the volume and the mass will be directly proportional. If two variables are directly proportional it means that the ratio of the variables will be the same. In this case it means that the ratio of the volumes of these solids will be the same as the ratio of the masses.

So we need to calculate the volume for each solid.

For the cone:
$$V = \frac{1}{3}\pi r^2 h$$
$$= \frac{1}{3}\pi \times 3^2 \times 12$$
$$= 36\pi$$

For the sphere:
$$V = \frac{4}{3}\pi r^3$$
$$= \frac{4}{3}\pi \times 3^3$$
$$= 36\pi$$

For the cylinder:
$$V = \pi r^2 h$$
$$= \pi \times 3^2 \times 12$$
$$= 108\pi$$

For the ratio:
$cone : sphere : cylinder$
$36\pi : 36\pi : 108\pi$
$\;\;1 \;\; : \;\; 1 \;\; : \;\; 3$

8 NUMBER CRUNCHING SOLUTIONS

1

The range is the difference between the highest and lowest values, but at this stage it does not tell us a specific value.

The median is in the 7 times table and this value is repeated to become the mode.

We do know that the fifth number is four times the second smallest number.

The mean is 11.2. From this we can calculate the total of the five numbers (N):

$$\frac{N}{5} = 11.2$$
$$N = 56$$

We now need to begin selecting numbers that may work.

Start with the median being equal to 7 and also include another 7 since this is the mode.

We cannot have any more prime numbers since 7 is prime.

The lowest value could be 1 since this is not prime meaning the highest is 18.

We have four numbers which sum to $1 + 7 + 7 + 18 = 33$. But $56 - 33 = 23$ so this is not possible since it is higher than 18.

| 1 | 7 | 7 | 18 | Not possible since other number would be 23. |

Now try the lowest value as 4 which means the largest value would be 21, keeping the two 7's. (We cannot try 2, 3 or 5 since these are primes.)

With these four values the sum is $4 + 7 + 7 + 21 = 39$. But $56 - 39 = 17$ which cannot work since there would be three prime numbers.

| 4 | 7 | 7 | 21 | Not possible since other number would be 17, another prime. |

Now try the lowest value as 6 which means the largest value would be 23 which cannot work since there would be three prime numbers.

| 6 | 7 | 7 | 23 |

So we now know that the multiple of 7 cannot be 7.

We will now try 14 as the median and include it twice in the calculations.

$14 + 14 = 28$ which means the remaining three values, two of which must be prime, must have a total of:
$56 - 28 = 28$.

One of these remaining three values must be four times the other, this means that the maximum value could be no more than 20, since $5 \times 4 = 20$.

If we used 24, that would mean the second number would be 6 and the sum would be above 28.

If 20 is the highest value then the lowest must be 3 for a range of 17.

The final number would be $28 - 20 - 3 = 5$.
Since 5 would be the second number and $20 = 4 \times 5$ we have found the set of numbers that satisfies all the requirements.

3   5   14   14   20

2

In the old system a person earning £32,000 would be taxed on the amount:
$32000 - 11500 = 20500$
£20,500 is taxed at 20%.
$20500 \times 0.2 = 4100$
The tax paid is £4,100.
In the new system the tax paid must be the same but it must be collected on all earnings above £12,000.
This means that tax is paid on $32000 - 12000 = 20000$.
Tax is paid on £20,000.
The percentage of this amount is given by:
$$\frac{4100}{20000} \times 100 = 20.5$$
The new standard rate will be 20.5%
This is the percentage required if earnings of £32,000 per year were to pay the same overall tax in the new system.

3

To be absolutely sure the submarine will not implode we will assume that the pressure increases by the maximum amount for every ten-metre descent.
The atmosphere is measured to the nearest 0.1. To find the upper bound we must halve this value and then add it to the rounded value:
$$\frac{0.1}{2} = 0.05$$
$1 + 0.05 = 1.05$
Now we divide the maximum number of atmospheres before implosion by this upper bound:
$$\frac{50}{1.05} = 47.62$$
This means that the submarine can descend by ten metres on 47.62 occasions. The depth reached will be:
$47.62 \times 10 = 476.2$
We can give the answer in metres rather than in tens of metres because the depth and the pressure were directly proportional.
The answer must be given to the nearest metre, so the submarine can descend no more than 476m to be absolutely sure it will not implode.

4

The minimum time possible will occur when the minimum words that can be read are used.
To find the lower bound on each of the given values we first look at what they are rounded to and then halve that value.
This means that $\frac{1000}{2} = 500$, $\frac{100}{2} = 50$ and $\frac{10}{2} = 5$.
We subtract each of these values from their respective rounded amounts to obtain:
$10000 - 500 = 9500$
$400 - 50 = 350$
$350 - 5 = 345$
To calculate the total number of words that need to be read we multiply all the lower bounds together:
$total\ words = 9500 \times 350 \times 345$
$\qquad\qquad\quad = 1147125000$

Number Crunching Solutions

The person can read 400 words per minute meaning the total number of minutes required would be:
$$\frac{1147125000}{400} = 2867812.5$$
The question requires the time in hours so we must divide by 60:
$$\frac{2867812.5}{60} = 47796.875$$
Rounded to the nearest hour we have 47,797 hours required to read all the words.

5

We need to calculate the cost over 20 years for each boiler to see if the savings made are greater than the initial cost of the boiler.
For the old boiler in one year:
The standing charges will be $30 \times 365 = 10950$
The unit charges will be $10000 \times 3 = 30000$
The total yearly cost will be $10950 + 30000 = 40950$
The yearly cost of the old boiler is £409.50
For the new boiler in one year:
The standing charges will be $25 \times 365 = 9125$
The unit charges will be $8000 \times 3.1 = 24800$ 80% of 10,000 is 8,000
The total yearly cost will be $9125 + 24800 = 33925$
The yearly cost of the old boiler is £339.25
The yearly saving is given by:
$409.50 - 339.25 - 70.25$
If we divide the cost of installing the boiler by the yearly saving this will indicate how many years are required to "get your money back":
$$\frac{1600}{70.25} = 22.78$$
This indicates that it would take nearly 23 years to cover the installation cost in savings.
The claim is not true.

6

The pressure formula is:
$$pressure = \frac{force}{area}$$
As with any formula, the units must be consistent. If the pressure was measured in newtons per square metre then the force must be in newtons and the area in square metres.
From the question we can calculate the pressure:
$$pressure = \frac{force}{area}$$
$$= \frac{4000}{0.1 \times 0.2}$$ The force on the ground was 4,000N and the rectangular area had sides of length 0.1m x 0.2m.
$$= 200000$$
The original pressure was 200,000N/m².
This pressure must remain the same with a new force applied of 3,200N.
We rearrange the formula to make area the subject:
$$pressure \times area = force$$
$$area = \frac{force}{pressure}$$
$$= \frac{3200}{200000}$$
$$= 0.016$$
The area required to maintain the same pressure is 0.016m².

GCSE Mathematics 9 – 1

7

To confirm the geography student's statement, we must assume the lowest number of doctors per square kilometre for Country A and the highest number of doctors per square kilometre for Country B. If Country A still has the highest number of doctors per square kilometre then the geography student is correct.
Doctors per square kilometre is found by dividing the number of doctors by the area of the country:
$$doctors\ per\ square\ km = \frac{number\ of\ doctors}{area\ of\ country}$$
To find the maximum value of a fraction we require the numerator to be the largest and the denominator to be the smallest.
To find the minimum value of a fraction we require the numerator to be the smallest and the denominator to be the largest.
The areas are given to the nearest 100km². To find the bounds we must halve this value to give 50. We then add or subtract this value to the areas as required.
The total number of doctors is given to the nearest 100. To find the bounds we must halve this value to give 50. We then add or subtract this value to the number of doctors as required.
The table below shows the upper and lower bounds for the values given.

	Country A	Country B
Area (km²) nearest 100km²	Lower Bound 669,950	Lower Bound 1,115,150
	Upper Bound 670,050	Upper Bound 1,115,250
Total doctors to nearest 100	Lower Bound 23,050	Lower Bound 38,450
	Upper Bound 23,150	Upper Bound 38,550

We need the lowest number for Country A:
$$doctors\ per\ square\ km = \frac{23050}{670050}$$
$$= 0.034400417$$
We need the highest number for country B:
$$doctors\ per\ square\ km = \frac{38550}{1115150}$$
$$= 0.03456934$$
We can see that:
$$doctors\ per\ square\ km\ Country\ B > doctors\ per\ square\ km\ Country\ A$$
$$0.0346 > 0.0344$$
The geography student cannot be certain of being correct.

8

To find the density of an object we require the mass and volume of the object. We then use the formula:
$$density = \frac{mass}{volume}$$
The goldfish bowl is in the shape of a sphere that is a mixture of glass and water. We must subtract the mass of the water from the mass of the goldfish bowl to find the mass of the glass.
The total volume of the goldfish bowl is:
$$V = \frac{4}{3}\pi r^3$$
$$= \frac{4}{3}\pi \times 15^3$$
$$= 4500\pi$$
The volume of the goldfish bowl is 4500π cm³
The mass of the goldfish bowl is given by:

Number Crunching Solutions

$$mass = density \times volume$$
$$= 1.1 \times 4500\pi$$
$$= 4950\pi$$

The mass of the goldfish bowl and water is 4950π grams.
The mass of the glass will be given by
$$mass\ of\ glass = mass\ of\ goldfish\ bowl - mass\ of\ water$$
$$= 4950\pi - 12000 \qquad\qquad \text{12kg is 12,000g}$$

Leave the units in this exact form until ready to calculate the final answer.

The density of the glass will be given by:
$$density = \frac{mass}{volume}$$
$$= \frac{4950\pi - 12000}{1420}$$
$$= 2.50$$

The density of the glass used is 2.50g/cm³ to three significant figures.

9

This question requires us to calculate the temperature of the greenhouse at the end of the 10 hours of warming.
We will then apply percentage multipliers to calculate the temperature of the greenhouse by 11p.m.
Rising 5°C for 10 hours means that the temperature rise will be $10 \times 5 = 50°C$.
So the temperature will be 60°C and this occurs at 6pm (ten hours after 8a.m.).
Between 6p.m. and 11p.m. there are five hours where the temperature reduces by 20% per hour. The multiplier for a 20% reduction is 0.8, and this will be applied five times to give the 11p.m. temperature.
$$60 \times 0.8^5 = 19.6608$$
The temperature to the nearest 0.1°C will be 19.7°C.

10

The smallest unit of time used in the question is seconds.
We will find the number of seconds that elapse between the times and then calculate how many degrees per second that the minute hand moves.
From 2hrs 26 minutes 36 seconds there are 33 minutes and 24 seconds until 3 o'clock.
Then there are a further 22 minutes and 30 seconds until 3hrs 22 minutes 30 seconds.
The time that elapses will be 55 minutes and 54 seconds.
The minute hand completes a full circle every 60 minutes.
This means that 360° are turned through in 60 minutes.
Dividing by 60 we find the minute hand turns through 6° every minute.
Dividing by 60 again we find that the minute hand turns through 0.1° every second.
Now we can total the angle moved through by the minute hand in 55 minutes and 54 seconds.
$$55 \times 6° + 54 \times 0.1° = 335.4°$$
The minute hand turns through 335.4° in the given time interval.

```
   33 minutes 24 seconds
+  22 minutes 30 seconds
   ─────────────────────
   55 minutes 54 seconds
```

11

The top 70% will be found by finding 30% on the cumulative frequency axis. This percentage corresponds to a grade number 4.
The top 20% will be found by finding 80% on the cumulative frequency axis. This percentage corresponds to a grade number 7.
We conclude that a grade C and a grade 4 are equivalent and that a grade A and a grade 7 are equivalent.

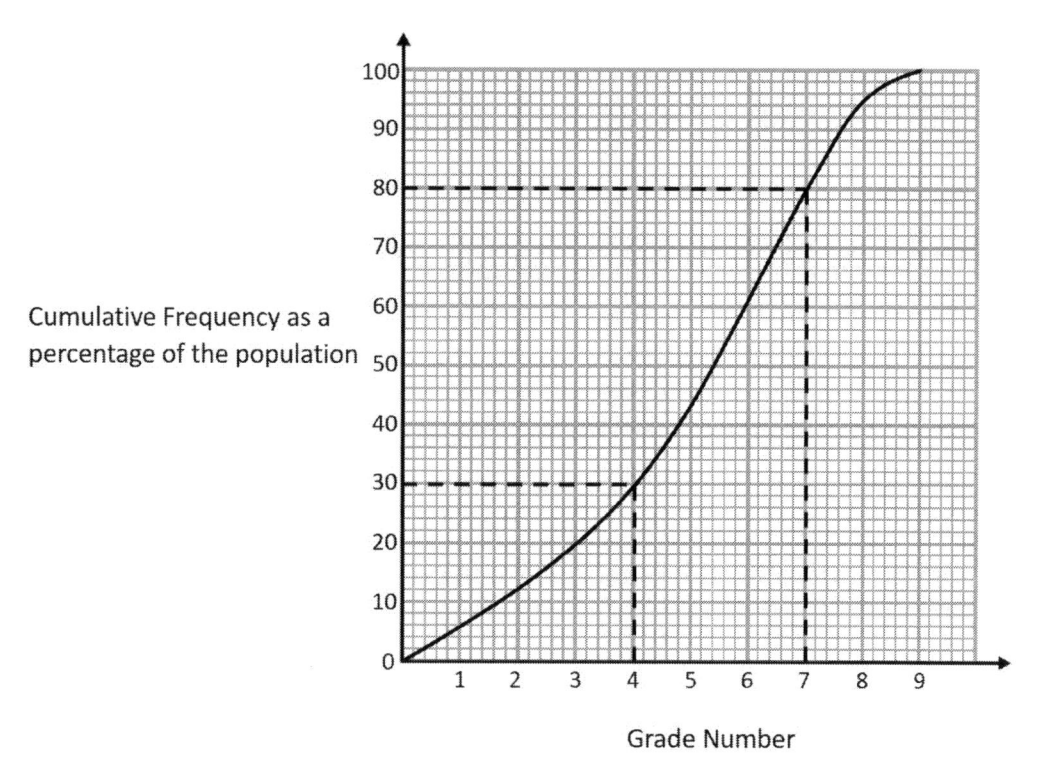

12

From the cumulative frequency graph we can find where the 80% boundary for the cumulative frequency would be (this will indicate the point where the top 20% of students begins).

We can see that there are 90 students in total. The top 20% will be give by $90 \times 0.8 = 72$.

We need to find 72 on the cumulative frequency axis.

This value corresponds to a mark of approximately 48 on the exam.

A mark of 48 out of 80 in percentage terms would be:

$$\frac{48}{80} \times 100 = 60\%$$

So the top 20% of students all got above 55% in the exam. From the information in the question this means that the top 10% of students will be awarded a level 7.

Since there were 90 students this means that 9 will be awarded a level 7.

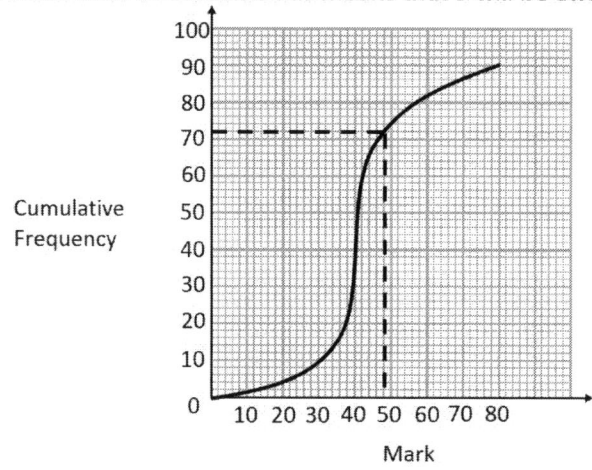

Number Crunching Solutions

13

Pressure is calculated using the following formula:
$$pressure = \frac{force}{area}$$
With any formula we must make sure the units we use are consistent.
We can measure the force in newtons and the area in square centimetres.
For the cuboid:
$$pressure = \frac{800}{20 \times 20}$$
$$= 2N/cm^2$$

For pressure calculations, only the area of the face in contact with the surface is required regardless of how the rest of the shape is constructed.

For the cylinder:
$$pressure = \frac{402}{\pi r^2}$$
$$= \frac{402}{\pi \times 8^2}$$
$$= 1.999N/cm^2$$

80mm is 8cm.

From the two values we can see that the cuboid exerts the greater pressure.

14

To calculate pressure we use the following formula:
$$pressure = \frac{force}{area}$$
We need the force and the area of each prism to find the pressures exerted on the table.
The area of the trapezium is given by:
$$area = \frac{1}{2}h(a+b)$$
$$= \frac{1}{2} \times 4 \times (2+6)$$
$$= 16$$
The trapezium has an area of 16cm².
The pressure exerted by the trapezoidal prism will be:
$$pressure = \frac{force}{area}$$
$$= \frac{17}{16}$$
$$= 1.0625$$
The trapezoidal prism exerts a pressure of 1.0625 newtons per square centimetre.
We need the area of the circle for the cylinder. The area will be given by πr^2.
We know the volume of the cylinder and must equate this to the general formula for the volume of a cylinder, $volume = \pi r^2 h$.
We then make πr^2 the subject to get the area.
$$volume = \pi r^2 h$$
$$180\pi = \pi r^2 \times 20 \quad \text{Divide by 20}$$
$$9\pi = \pi r^2$$

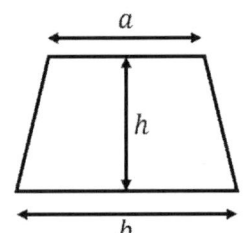

The area of the circle is $9\pi cm^2$.
The pressure exerted by the cylinder will be:
$$pressure = \frac{force}{area}$$
$$= \frac{30}{9\pi}$$
$$= 1.061$$
Since $1.0625 > 1.061$ we conclude that the trapezoidal prism exerts the greater pressure.

15

There are two components to the amount the government will fund. The first is the fixed £2,500 and the second is the percentage of the purchase price of the electric car.
If the mean value of the electric car is £28,000 then 20% of this value will be:
$28000 \times 0.2 = 5600$
20% of £28,000 is £5,600.
The total government funding per car will be:
$5600 + 2500 = 8100$
The funding per car is £8,100.
If the total budget is £500 million then the number of electric cars that can be funded will be:
$$\frac{500000000}{8100} = 61728$$
The government scheme will fund up to 61,728 electric cars.

16

The insurance pay out must be greater than £150 for a purchased item.
If we call the price P of the purchased item we can write an inequality.
The multiplier for a 20% reduction is 0.8, if this reduction is applied in three successive years the multiplier will be 0.8^3.
The inequality becomes:
$$P \times 0.8^3 > 150$$
$$P > \frac{150}{0.8^3}$$
$$P > 292.96875$$
$$P \geq 292.97$$
The purchase price must be at least £292.97 if the pay out is to exceed the insurance cover after breaking the device at the end of three years.

17

The prime numbers less than 20 are:
2,3,5,7,11,13,17,19
There are eight primes less than 20.
The number of odd numbers less than 48 is given by halving the value:
$$\frac{48}{2} = 24$$
There are 24 odd numbers less than 48.
Multiplying these values together gives:
$8 \times 24 = 192$

The square numbers less than 200 are:
1,4,9,16,25,36,49,64,81,100,121,144,169,196
There are 14 square numbers less than 200.
The first positive even number is two.
$14^2 = 196$

Since $196 > 192$ we conclude that the second value is the largest.

18

This is a proportion based problem.
We need to establish what area of the painting will require red paint and what area will require other colours.

Number Crunching Solutions

Since the paint costs can be priced on square centimetres we will convert the measurements of the painting into centimetres and find the area:
$200 \times 300 = 60000$
The total area of the painting is 60,000cm².
Eight percent will be red:
$60000 \times 0.08 = 4800$
The artist requires 4,800cm² of red paint.
The remaining area will be other colours:
$60000 - 4800 = 55200$
The remaining area is 55,200cm².
The cost of the red paint was priced per square inch so we need to convert square centimetres to square inches:

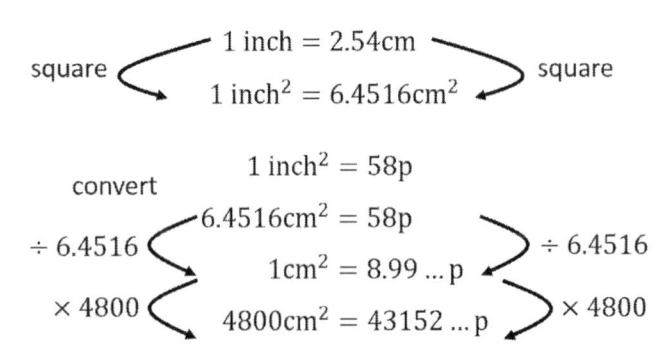

square ⟷ 1 inch = 2.54cm ⟷ square
1 inch² = 6.4516cm²

convert
÷ 6.4516 — 1 inch² = 58p — ÷ 6.4516
6.4516cm² = 58p
1cm² = 8.99…p
× 4800 — 4800cm² = 43152…p — × 4800

The cost of the red paint will be £431.52.
The remaining area is paint of different colours and this is priced per square centimetre.
The cost of the remaining paint will be given by:

× 5520 — 45p = 10cm² — × 5520
248400p = 55200cm²

The remaining cost will be £2,484.
The total cost will be:
$431.52 + 2484 = 2915.52$
The paint costs are £2,915.52.

19

The scale relates the model size to the real-world size.
From the ratio we can see that the real-world size is 76 times larger.
If the model travels at 8cm per second then we can multiply this value by 76 to get the real-world speed.
$8 \times 76 = 608$
The train travels at 608cm per second in the real world. This is 6.08m/s.
We now need to convert the distance and time measurements:
The seconds must be converted to hours.
One hour is 3,600 seconds, so we can multiply by 3,600:
$6.08 \times 3600 = 21888$
The real train would travel 21,888m in 3,600 seconds (or one hour).
We now convert this distance into kilometres by dividing by 1,000:
$$\frac{21888}{1000} = 21.888$$

GCSE Mathematics 9 – 1

The real train travels at 21.888km/h.
We now divide by 1.6 to convert kilometres into miles:
$$\frac{21.888}{1.6} = 13.68$$
The real train travels at 13.68mph.

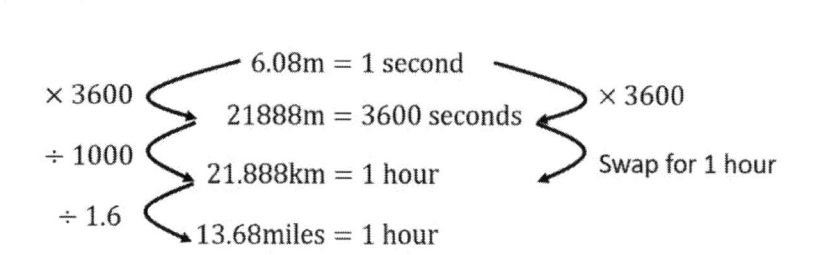

× 3600 ⟶ 6.08m = 1 second ⟶ × 3600
  21888m = 3600 seconds
÷ 1000
  21.888km = 1 hour ⟶ Swap for 1 hour
÷ 1.6
  13.68miles = 1 hour

20

For the first cheese we need to relate the volume of the cylinder to the given cost.
The first cheese has a volume given by:
$$volume = \pi r^2 h$$
$$= \pi \times 4^2 \times 10$$
$$= 160\pi$$
We can say that 160πcm³ costs £10.
Since the price is directly proportional to volume we can calculate the cost for 200cm³:

÷ 160π ⟶ 160πcm³ = £10 ⟶ ÷ 160π
  $1cm^3 = £\frac{10}{160\pi}$
× 200 ⟶ $200cm^3 = £\frac{10}{160\pi} \times 200$ ⟶ × 200

From the proportion calculation we can see that 200cm³ of the first cheese costs £3.98.

We now need to calculate the surface area of a 200cm³ sphere.
Volume is given by:
$$volume = \frac{4}{3}\pi r^3$$
$$\frac{4}{3}\pi r^3 = 200$$
$4\pi r^3 = 600$ Multiply by 3.
$\pi r^3 = 150$ Divide by 4.
$r^3 = \frac{150}{\pi}$ Divide by π.
$r = \sqrt[3]{\frac{150}{\pi}}$ Cube root.

Now we calculate the surface area of a 200cm³ sphere:
$$surface\ area = 4\pi r^2$$
$$= 4\pi \left(\sqrt[3]{\frac{150}{\pi}}\right)^2$$

Leave the answer in this form for the moment as we only need to declare the final rounded answer.
Now we can relate this area with the given costs:

Relate the area of the second cheese with the cost to find how much £1 will buy.
Then relate the area of the 200cm³ cheese with the cost:

Number Crunching Solutions

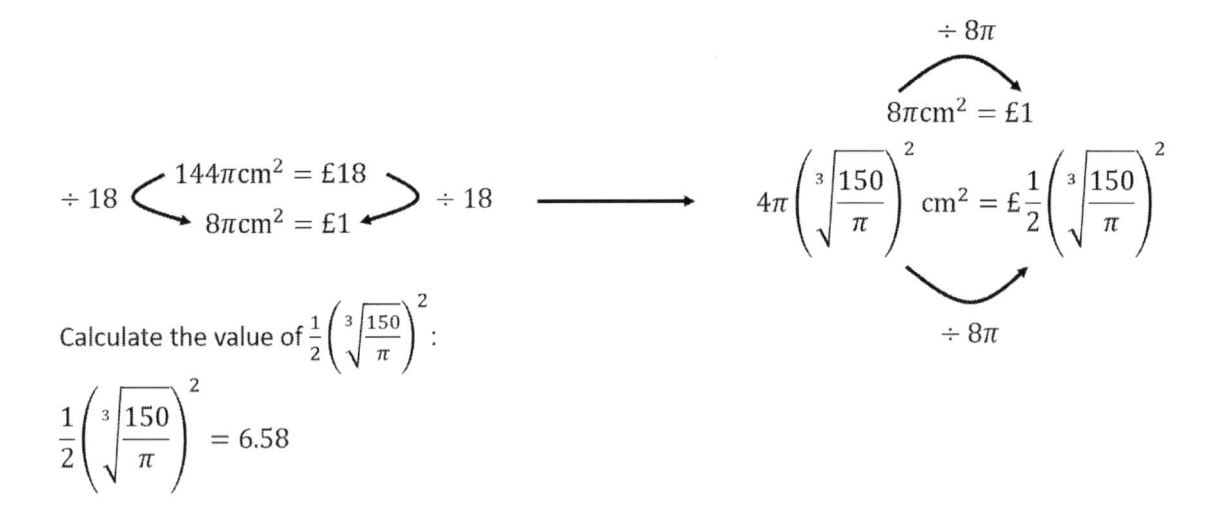

$$\div 18 \underset{8\pi cm^2 = £1}{\overset{144\pi cm^2 = £18}{\longleftrightarrow}} \div 18 \longrightarrow 4\pi\left(\sqrt[3]{\frac{150}{\pi}}\right)^2 cm^2 = £\frac{1}{2}\left(\sqrt[3]{\frac{150}{\pi}}\right)^2 \quad \overset{\div 8\pi}{\underset{\div 8\pi}{8\pi cm^2 = £1}}$$

Calculate the value of $\frac{1}{2}\left(\sqrt[3]{\frac{150}{\pi}}\right)^2$:

$$\frac{1}{2}\left(\sqrt[3]{\frac{150}{\pi}}\right)^2 = 6.58$$

From the proportion calculation we can see that 200cm³ of the second cheese costs £6.58.
We can conclude that the first cheese would cost the least for 200cm³ since £3.98 is less than £6.58

21

We need to examine all the square numbers less than 100.
Then we need to add or subtract three to the square numbers.
We check if the number has the digit "one" contained in it.
We order all the numbers identified and select the middle value to obtain the median.

The square numbers are:
1,4,9,16,25,36,49,64,81

We now add and subtract three to each square number to obtain:
−2,4,1,7,6,12,13,19,22,28,33,39,46,52,61,67,78,84

The numbers with digit "one", in order are:
1,12,13,19,61

The median is 13.

22

The general formula to calculate percentage error is given by:
$$percentage\ error = \frac{real\ value - estimate}{real\ value} \times 100$$
The area of a circle is given by $area = \pi r^2$.
The percentage error will be:
$$percentage\ error = \frac{\pi r^2 - \sqrt[3]{40 - \sqrt{80}}(r^2)}{\pi r^2} \times 100$$
$$= \frac{\pi \times 5^2 - \sqrt[3]{40 - \sqrt{80}}(5^2)}{\pi \times 5^2} \times 100$$
$$= -0.053\%$$
The percentage error is 0.053% correct to two significant figures. You can ignore the negative sign.

GCSE Mathematics 9 – 1

23

You will need to use your calculator to answer this question.
The idea of an iteration is that you use your previous answer to obtain successively more accurate approximations.
If we want the answer to two decimal places, we must get two successive answers that agree to the same two decimal places.
To begin we substitute $x_1 = 2.5$ into the formula.
On your calculator type "2.5" and then press "equals". This means that the calculator has stored the previous answer in its memory.
The following are the instructions for a CASIO calculator.
Now in your calculator type:
Square root
Open bracket
Three
Minus
Fraction button
One
Down arrow
Ans
Right arrow
Close bracket
Equals
After this you can keep pressing equals and recording your answers as you go. When you obtain two successive answers that agree to two decimal places you stop.
The full calculation is shown below.

$$x_{n+1} = \sqrt{3 - \frac{1}{x_n}}$$

$$x_2 = \sqrt{3 - \frac{1}{x_1}}$$
$$= \sqrt{3 - \frac{1}{2.5}}$$
$$= 1.61245155$$
$$= 1.61$$

$$x_3 = \sqrt{3 - \frac{1}{x_2}}$$
$$= \sqrt{3 - \frac{1}{1.61245155}}$$
$$= 1.542668573$$
$$= 1.54$$

$$x_4 = \sqrt{3 - \frac{1}{x_3}}$$
$$= \sqrt{3 - \frac{1}{1.542668573}}$$
$$= 1.533549029$$
$$= 1.53$$

$$x_5 = \sqrt{3 - \frac{1}{x_4}}$$
$$= \sqrt{3 - \frac{1}{1.533549029}}$$
$$= 1.532291688$$
$$= 1.53$$

The last two answers agree to two decimal places: the answer is 1.53.

24

From the incomplete Venn diagram we can say that the total who own a Mobile Phone or a Tablet PC must be 90 since 10 do not own either.

Number Crunching Solutions

The pie charts show the proportion of people who own each item.
For the Mobile Phone pie chart we can calculate how many people own a Mobile Phone:
$$\frac{306}{360} \times 100 = 85$$
85 people own a Mobile Phone.
For the Tablet PC pie chart we can calculate how many people own a Tablet PC:
$$\frac{198}{360} \times 100 = 55$$
55 people own a Tablet PC.
We can use this information to calculate the "overlap" in the Venn diagram. That is, the people who owned both a Mobile Phone and a Tablet PC:
$$85 + 55 = 140$$
Since there can only be 90 people inside this area we can see that the overlap is:
$$140 - 90 = 50$$
This means that 50 people must own both a Mobile Phone and a Tablet PC.
This is because the overlap is counted twice when adding 85 and 55.

We know that 85 people own a Mobile Phone. Since 50 are in the overlap this means that:
$$85 - 50 = 35$$
There are 35 people who own a Mobile Phone only.

We know that 55 people own a Tablet PC. Since 50 are in the overlap this means that:
$$55 - 50 = 5$$
There are 5 people who own a Tablet PC only.

We can now complete the Venn Diagram.

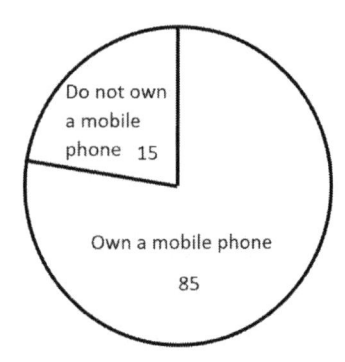

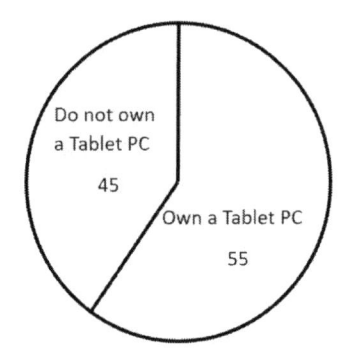

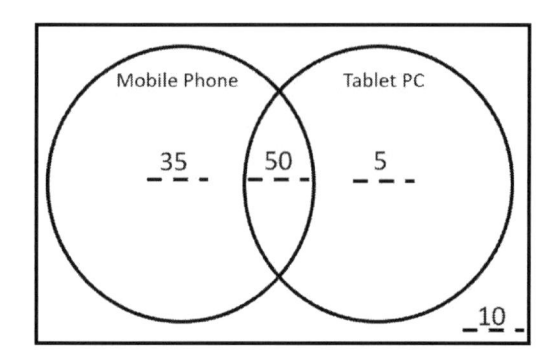

(Pie chart: Do not own a mobile phone 15; Own a mobile phone 85)

(Pie chart: Do not own a Tablet PC 45; Own a Tablet PC 55)

(Venn diagram: Mobile Phone 35, overlap 50, Tablet PC 5, outside 10)

25

If each successive term is the sum of the previous two terms, you are dealing with a Fibonacci sequence.
We know that the growth on day four and day five will be equal to the growth on day six. From this we can write:
$$day\ 4 + day\ 5 = day\ 6$$
$$11 + day\ 5 = 29$$
$$day\ 5 = 18$$
We can now complete the sequence going backwards to day two:
$$day\ 3 = day\ 5 - day\ 4$$
$$= 18 - 11$$
$$= 7$$
$$day\ 2 = day\ 4 - day\ 3$$
$$= 11 - 7$$
$$= 4$$
The weed grew 4mm on day two.

GCSE Mathematics 9 – 1

26

If the man has eaten 100g of Butter A then he has consumed 2g of salt since Butter A has 1g of salt per 50g of butter.
The remaining salt allowance would be $6 - 2 = 4$g of salt.
This extra 4g must come from 32g of Butter B.
From this we can see that 1g of salt is contained in every 8g of Butter B.
If we divide 50 by 8 we will find the salt content per 50g of Butter B:
$$\frac{50}{8} = 6.25$$
Butter B has 6.25g of salt per 50g of butter.

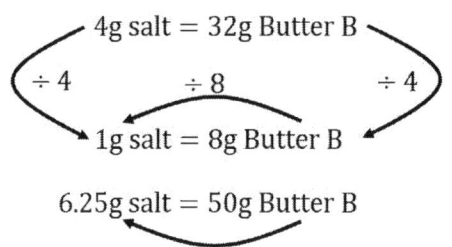

4g salt = 32g Butter B
$\div 4$ $\div 8$ $\div 4$
1g salt = 8g Butter B

6.25g salt = 50g Butter B
$\div 8$

27

We know the accuracy of the 20:00 time, it is to the nearest two hours.
We require the earlier time for this question to get the shortest time interval.
If a value is given to the nearest 2, we halve this value to obtain 1 and then we can subtract this value from the value given to get the lower bound.
In this case 1 represents one hour.
The earliest time would have been 19:00.
The shortest time interval was five and three-quarter hours.
If we subtract this time from 19:00 we obtain 13:15.
This means that the upper bound of the 13:00 time was 13:15.
This is 15 minutes greater which would have represented half of the accuracy level.
$15 \times 2 = 30$
The 13:00 time must have been to the nearest 30 minutes.

28

Call the fuel consumption for a journey of 480 miles at 200mph x litres.
The fuel consumption at 400mph will then be $1.5x$ litres since this is 50% greater.
We will also use x litres to represent a full tank of fuel for the plane.
We can say that:

$$x \text{ litres} = 480 \text{ miles} \qquad \text{at 200mph}$$

But since the plane only has x litres of fuel available when travelling at 400mph we can say that:

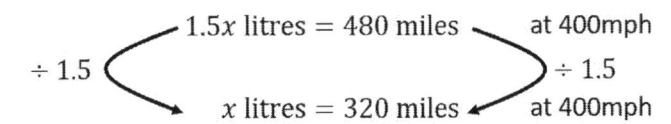

$1.5x$ litres = 480 miles   at 400mph
$\div 1.5$ $\div 1.5$
x litres = 320 miles   at 400mph

From this we can see that the plane could travel 320 miles at 400mph.

29

First point:
The median is the middle value of ordered data.
We need to find the total number of students that took part in the test.
$8 + 16 + 24 + 24 + 8 = 80$
The median will lie between the 40th and 41st individuals.
These individuals are in the $20 \leq m < 30$ interval since the cumulative total less than 30 will be:
$8 + 16 + 24 = 48$

Number Crunching Solutions

Since we only know the range of values in this interval and not the individual results we cannot be certain that the median will be 26 or 27.
If we were to use proportion, we can say that the 40th student will be the 16th individual in the $20 \leq m < 30$ interval. There are 24 students in this interval and $\frac{16}{24} = \frac{2}{3}$. This means that we could estimate the median as being $\frac{2}{3}$ of the distance into this interval.
The interval width is 10 and $\frac{2}{3}$ of 10 is between 6 or 7.
This would mean a mark of 26 or 27 which is what the professor predicted.
This can only remain a prediction however since we do not know exact values.

Interval	$0 \leq m < 10$	$10 \leq m < 20$	$20 \leq m < 30$	$30 \leq m < 40$	$40 \leq m \leq 50$
Number of Students	8	16	24	24	8
Running Total	8	24	48	72	80

The median is $\frac{2}{3}$ of the distance in the $20 \leq m < 30$ interval.

Second point:
80 students took the test. The test had a total of 50 marks available.
The number of marks to get 20% would be:
$0.2 \times 50 = 10$
The number of students who got less than 10 marks was eight.
The number of marks to get 80% would be:
$0.8 \times 50 = 40$
The number of students who got 40 marks or more was eight.
The professor claimed that the number who attained less than 20% would be equal to those who attained 80% or more. The number of students for each of these was eight. The professor was correct.

Third point:
The range is the difference between the highest and lowest mark.
We cannot calculate this accurately because we do not know the exact marks that students achieved. We can only give an estimate as to what values the range lies between. The maximum range will be given if a student scored zero marks and another scored 50 marks. This is possible given that zero and 50 can be attained. We can say that the range will have a maximum value of:
$50 - 0 = 50$.
The minimum range can be found by letting the lowest mark be 9 from the $0 \leq m < 10$ interval (10 is not allowed). The highest mark could be 40 from the $40 \leq m \leq 50$ interval. This would give a minimum range of:
$40 - 9 = 31$
All we can say is that the students' marks had a range between 31 and 50 inclusive.
We cannot be sure that the range was 50.
The professor could be correct but we are not certain.

30

We must calculate the cost of the cereal, butter and eggs. Then we can subtract this value and the £2.40 from £12 to find what the correct price of the milk would have been. We will then calculate what proportion the milk has been increased by and apply this to the whole bill.
For the cereal:
750g costs £2 so 1,500g will cost £4.
For the butter:
500g costs £2.50.

For the eggs:
12 eggs cost £1.50.
These thee items have a total of:
$4 + 2.5 + 1.5 = 8$
We can now subtract £8 and £2.40 from £12 to find the correct milk price:
$12 - 8 - 2.4 = 1.6$
The correct price for the four pints purchased was £1.60.
The bill on the receipt for these four pints would have been £4 since the bill was £2.40 too much.
The proportion that the milk was increased by is:
$$\frac{4}{1.6} = 2.5$$
The original correct bill would have been £9.60.
If we multiply this by 2.5 we will have the price for all four items if they were all incorrectly increased by the same proportion as the milk:
$9.6 \times 2.5 = 24$
The bill would have been £24.

31

Note that x is given as a percentage. When used in calculations as a percentage multiplier we will need to divide by 100 to give $\frac{x}{100}$.
From the information in the question we can write:

$$900000 \times 0.8 \times \frac{x}{100} = 504000 \qquad \text{We require } x\% \text{ of 80\% of 900,000.}$$
$$\frac{720000x}{100} = 504000 \qquad \text{Multiply } 900000 \times 0.8 \text{ and write the value on the numerator.}$$
$$7200x = 504000 \qquad \text{Simplify the fraction.}$$
$$x = 70 \qquad \text{Divide by 7200.}$$

The value of x is 70.

32

To see if Cumbria can reach 1 million people first we will assume that Cumbria has the largest starting population and Dorset and Worcestershire have the smallest starting population. All the populations are given to the nearest 100,000.
To find the bounds we need to halve this value:
$$\frac{100000}{2} = 50000$$
We now add this value to the population of Cumbria:
$500000 + 50000 = 550000$
We subtract this value from the population of Dorset:
$800000 - 50000 = 750000$
We also subtract this value from the population of Worcestershire:
$700000 - 50000 = 650000$
We can now apply percentage multipliers to each population to see which will reach 1 million first.
The percentage increases are small so it may be worth using powers to get a ball park figure as to how many years it will take. All answers are given to the nearest whole number.
For Cumbria:
$550000 \times 1.05^{10} = 895892$
This is not enough.
$550000 \times 1.05^{12} = 987721$
Nearly enough.
$550000 \times 1.05^{13} = 1037107$

Number Crunching Solutions

It could take Cumbria as little as 13 years to reach 1 million people.

For Dorset, we only need to do one calculation using a 2% increase multiplier of 1.02:
$750000 \times 1.02^{13} = 970205$
Since this is still less than 1 million we conclude that Cumbria could reach 1 million people before Dorset.
For Worcestershire, we also only need one calculation using a 3% increase multiplier of 1.03:
$650000 \times 1.03^{13} = 954547$
Since this is still less than 1 million we conclude that Cumbria could reach 1 million people before Worcestershire.
Overall, it is possible that Cumbria could reach 1 million people before Dorset and Worcestershire.

33

If five friends are to divide a cake into five equal sectors, then the angle of each sector that each friend should receive will be:
$$\frac{360°}{5} = 72°$$
All angles are measured to the nearest degree ($1°$).
To find the smallest remaining piece of cake we will assume that each of the four friends took the largest sector. This means we need the upper bound for each sector.
Since each angle is measured to the nearest $1°$, we halve this value to give $0.5°$.
We now add this value to the sector angle to give the maximum angle possible:
$72° + 0.5° = 72.5°$
If four friends took sectors with this angle, the angle used would be:
$72.5° \times 4 = 290°$
This leaves:
$360° - 290° = 70°$
The remaining sector would be $70°$.
The fraction of the cake left for the fifth friend would be $\frac{70°}{360°}$.

This simplifies to give $\frac{7}{36}$.

34

For this question we need to calculate:
- The volume of each container
- The volume of each screw
- The number of screws that fit in each container
- The cost of making each container
- The profit made by selling each container

The units for the screw were in millimetres; we will convert this to centimetres for consistency:
50mm is 5cm and 10mm is 1cm. Each screw is treated as a cuboid when packaged into the containers.
With any question where you are fitting a two-or three-dimensional object into another, you must make sure that the smaller object will fit an exact multiple of times into the larger object. We do this by looking at the dimensions of each object. The screw is a cuboid with dimensions 1cm, 1cm and 5cm. Each of these values (1 and 5) are factors of the dimensions of the containers, 5cm, 10cm, 15cm and 20cm. This means that regardless of how the screws are packed into the containers, it is possible to completely fill the containers without any overlap or space left over. With this fact established, we can divide the volume of each container by the volume of the screw to find the number of screws that would fit into that container.

For Container A:
$$\begin{aligned}volume &= length \times width \times height \\ &= 20 \times 5 \times 10 \\ &= 1000\end{aligned}$$

The volume of Container A is 1,000cm³.
It costs 1p for every 50cm³ of volume so we can calculate the cost of manufacturing Container A:
$$cost = \frac{1000}{50}$$
$$= 20$$
It costs 20p to manufacture Container A.
For Container B:
$$volume = length \times width \times height$$
$$= 15 \times 10 \times 10$$
$$= 1500$$
The volume of Container B is 1,500cm³.
It costs 1p for every 50cm³ of volume so we can calculate the cost of manufacturing Container B:
$$cost = \frac{1500}{50}$$
$$= 30$$
It costs 30p to manufacture Container B.

The volume of the screw:
$$volume = length \times width \times height$$
$$= 5 \times 1 \times 1$$
$$= 5$$
Each screw has a volume of 5cm³.
Now we calculate how many screws fit into each container by dividing the container volume by the screw volume.
Container A:
$$number\ of\ screws = \frac{1000}{5}$$
$$= 200$$
You can fit 200 screws into Container A.
Container B:
$$number\ of\ screws = \frac{1500}{5}$$
$$= 300$$
You can fit 300 screws into Container B.
The manufacturer makes a profit of 2p per screw sold.
We can now calculate the profit made on each container.

Container A:
$$profit = income - expenses$$
$$= 200 \times 2 - 20$$
$$= 400 - 20$$
$$= 380$$
The manufacturer makes a profit of 380p for each Container A sold.
Container B:
$$profit = income - expenses$$
$$= 300 \times 2 - 30$$
$$= 600 - 30$$
$$= 570$$
The manufacturer makes a profit of 570p for each Container B sold.
The extra profit on Container B:
$570 - 380 = 190$
The extra profit made is 190p.

9 GEOMETRY SOLUTIONS

1

The scaled down city will fit into the circular card if the diagonal of the city rectangle is no longer than the diameter of the circle.
The diagonal of the city can be found using Pythagoras:
$$a^2 + b^2 = c^2$$
$$10^2 + 12^2 = c^2$$
$$100 + 144 = c^2$$
$$c^2 = 244$$
$$c = \sqrt{244}$$
$$= 15.62 \ldots$$
The units here are kilometres.
The scale of the jigsaw is 1:50,000.
The diameter of the circle is 32cm which is double the given radius of 16cm.
We can multiply the diameter by 50,000 to find the real distance in centimetres:
$32 \times 50000 = 1600000$cm
We now divide by 100 to find this distance in metres:
$$\frac{1600000}{100} = 16000 \text{m}$$
We divide by 1,000 to find this distance in kilometres:
$$\frac{16000}{1000} = 16 \text{km}$$
$16 > 15.62$
This means that the city will fit into the circle jigsaw.

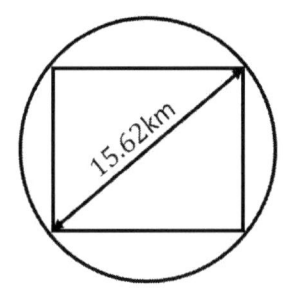

2

The distance between the supports is the same as the base of the trapezium.
This base can be split into three sections:
The first will be 12m and the other two will be the base of the right-angled triangles shown. These right-angled triangles are identical because the bridge is symmetrical about the vertical axis. We can find the unknown side using Pythagoras:

GCSE Mathematics 9 – 1

$a^2 + b^2 = c^2$
$a^2 + 4^2 = 5^2$
$\quad a^2 = 5^2 - 4^2$
$\quad\quad = 9$
$\quad a = 3$ Square root.

The base of the right-angled triangle is 3.
The total support distance will be:
$support\ distance = 3 + 12 + 3$
$\quad\quad\quad\quad\quad\quad\quad = 18$

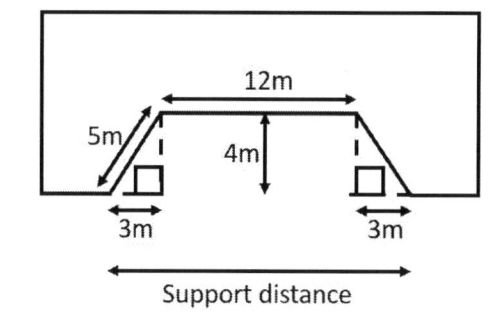

$18 < 20$
Therefore, the bridge will be stable.

3

This is a loci-construction problem. With construction problems we must recognise how a requirement in the question tells us which construction to do. You cannot use a protractor in this question.

When you need to find the locus of points that are nearer to one line than another, in this case closer to the road AB than the road AC, we need to construct an "angle bisector" at A.

When you need to find the locus of points that are the same distance from two points, in this case the same distance from A and C, we need to construct a "perpendicular bisector".

We will begin by constructing the angle bisector at A.

For this construction you must keep the compass set at the same length throughout.

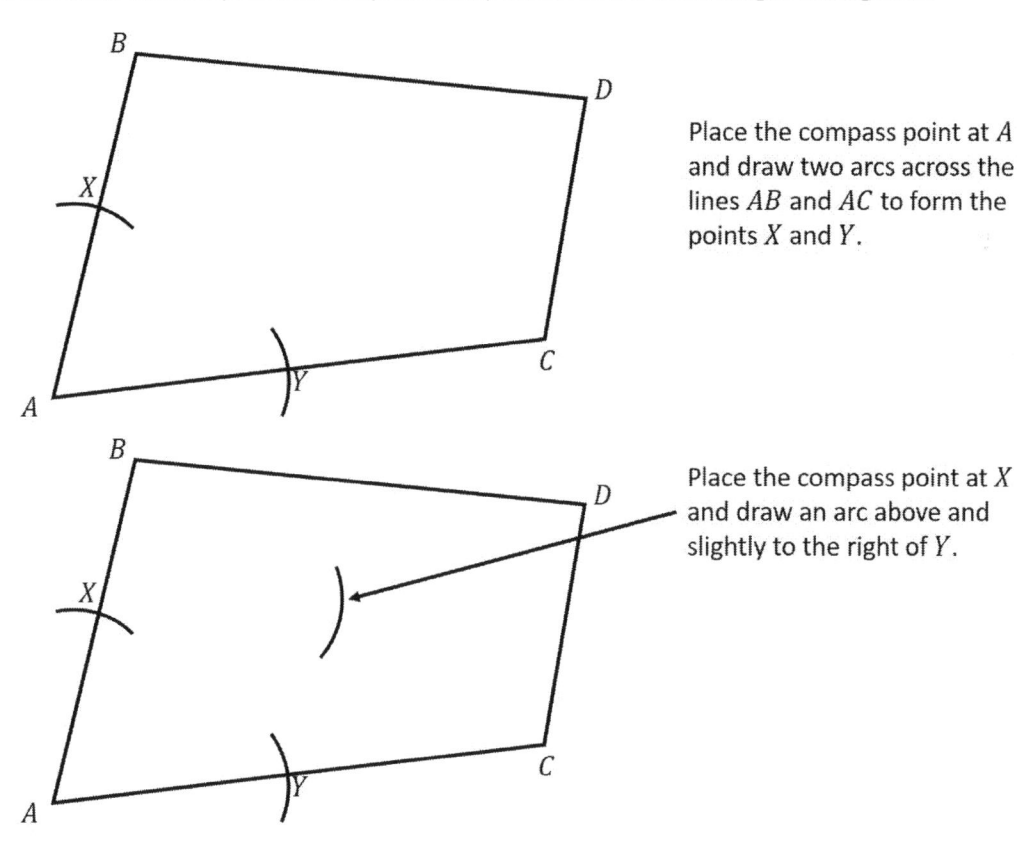

Place the compass point at A and draw two arcs across the lines AB and AC to form the points X and Y.

Place the compass point at X and draw an arc above and slightly to the right of Y.

85

Geometry Solutions

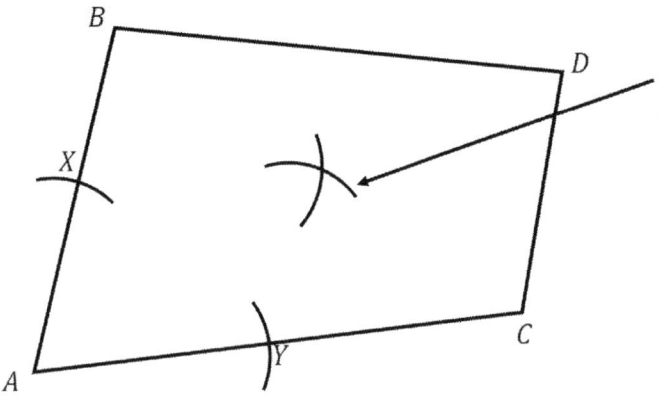

Place the compass point at Y and draw an arc through the arc you drew from X.

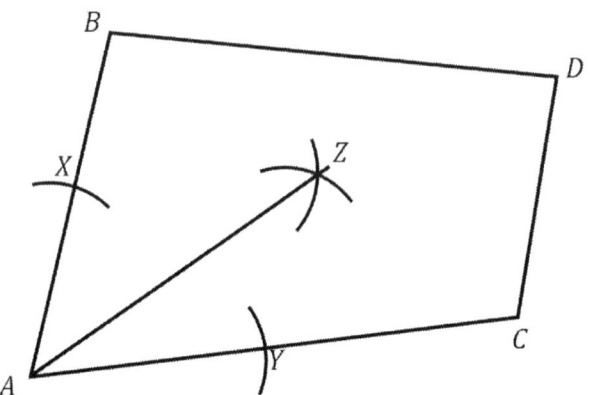

Draw a line from A to the point of intersection of the arcs at Z.

This line is the angle bisector. The TV mast must be closer to AB so we require the "AB" side of the angle bisector line.

We now construct the perpendicular bisector of the line AC.
We will construct a perpendicular bisector assuming there is not much space for the construction.

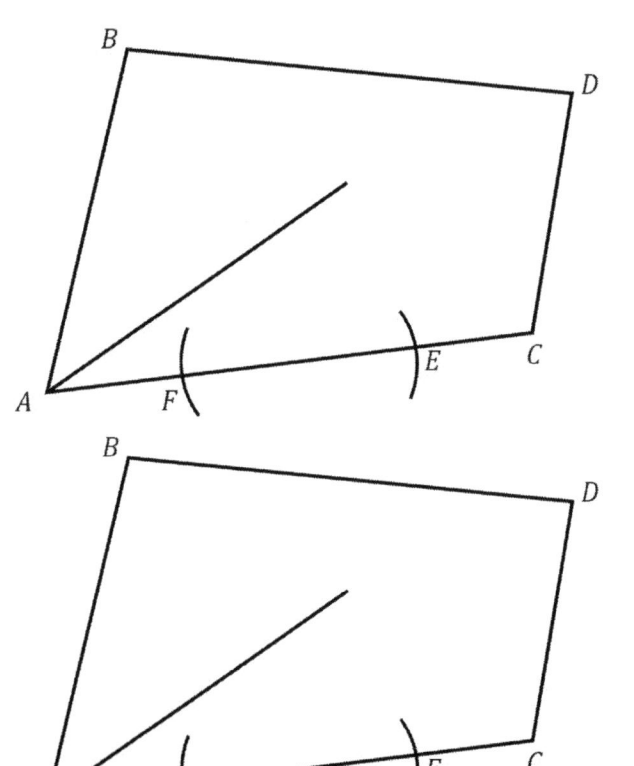

The construction lines have been removed on this diagram.
Only the angle bisector is shown.

For the perpendicular bisector, set the compass length to about three quarters the length of AC.

Place the point at A and cross the line AC. This is shown at point E.

Place the point at C and cross the line AC. This is shown at the point F.

Set the compass length to FE and maintain this for the rest of the construction.

GCSE Mathematics 9 – 1

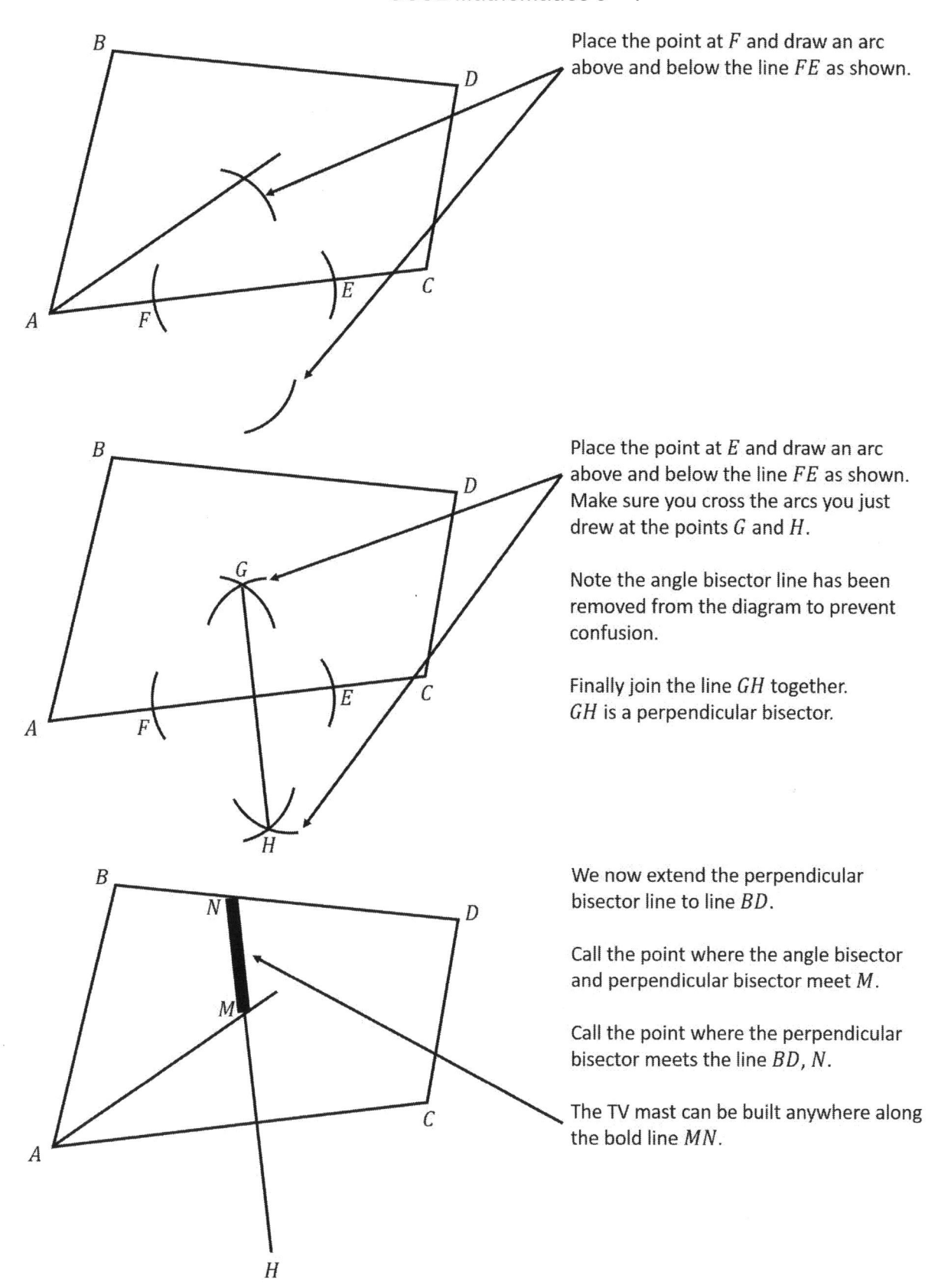

Place the point at F and draw an arc above and below the line FE as shown.

Place the point at E and draw an arc above and below the line FE as shown. Make sure you cross the arcs you just drew at the points G and H.

Note the angle bisector line has been removed from the diagram to prevent confusion.

Finally join the line GH together. GH is a perpendicular bisector.

We now extend the perpendicular bisector line to line BD.

Call the point where the angle bisector and perpendicular bisector meet M.

Call the point where the perpendicular bisector meets the line BD, N.

The TV mast can be built anywhere along the bold line MN.

The bold line shows the locus of points that are nearer to road AB than the road AC and are the same distance from the points A and C.

Geometry Solutions

4

An invariant point is one that does not change location (coordinates) under a given transformation. If you are given a single point that must remain invariant then you can apply enlargements, rotations or reflections and all can be used to make a single point invariant.

When two points must remain invariant there are less options available. The best option is to use a reflection in a line that passes through the two given points. Since the points lie on the mirror line they will not change under a reflection.

This means we need to find an equation of a line that passes through A and B.

A straight line has the general equation $y = mx + c$ where m is the gradient and c the y-intercept.

We can find m by using the two given coordinates of A and B. The gradient is found by dividing the difference in the y values by the difference in the x values.

$$m = \frac{6-4}{5-4}$$
$$= 2$$

The equation will be $y = 2x + c$.

To find c we need to substitute one of the given coordinates on the line into the equation and then solve for c. We will use (4,4).

$4 = 2(4) + c$
$ = 8 + c$ Subtract 8 and reverse the equation.
$c = -4$

The full equation of the straight line through A and B is $y = 2x - 4$.

The required transformation is a reflection in the line $y = 2x - 4$.

An alternative could have been to use an enlargement of scale factor one.

5

The ratios can be used to find the length scale factor (LSF).

The LSF will be:
$$\frac{50000}{20000} = 2.5$$

This means that the lengths on the road map will appear 2.5 times larger than those on the tourist map.

We require the area scale factor (ASF) to find the ratio of areas.

The ASF is related to the LSF by the formula:

$ASF = LSF^2$
$ = 2.5^2$
$ = 6.25$

This means the forested area on the road map will be 6.25 times greater than that on the tourist map.

We can now write the ratio as required:

$tourist\ map\ area : road\ map\ area$
$1 : 6.25$ Multiply by 4 to remove a 0.25 for an integer answer.
$4 : 25$

6

The important points in this question are the parallel lines and the use of a scale factor.

We are given the area scale factor (ASF) from the triangle ABC to triangle ADE.

We need to find the side lengths of the larger triangle in terms of the vectors a and b.

This means we require the length scale factor (LSF).

The LSF and ASF are related by the following formula:

$area\ scale\ factor = length\ scale\ factor^2$
$ASF = LSF^2$

If $ASF = 9$, then:
$LSF = \sqrt{9}$
$= 3$

The larger triangle ADE has side lengths that are three times the length of the smaller triangle ABC.
We can now write the vector equation to find the vector $\vec{AE}$:

$\vec{AE} = \vec{AD} + \vec{DE}$
$= 3\vec{AB} + 3\vec{BC}$
$= 3\boldsymbol{a} + 3\boldsymbol{b}$

Write vector equations like you are planning a route from one point to another. In this case you are going from A to E via D. So the separate vectors for each section of the journey must be written down and added: $\vec{AE} = \vec{AD} + \vec{DE}$

The answer is $3\boldsymbol{a} + 3\boldsymbol{b}$.

7

This question requires knowledge of which type of transformation can change the area of an object.
There are four transformations:
- Rotation
- Reflection
- Enlargement
- Translation

Only enlargement can change the area of the shape. The other three change the orientation or location of the shape but not the area. We are interested in the enlargement of scale factor 2.
An enlargement scale factor is the same as a length scale factor (LSF). The LSF is related to the area scale factor (ASF) by the following formula:

$area\ scale\ factor = length\ scale\ factor^2$
$ASF = LSF^2$
$= 2^2$
$= 4$

So the ASF is 4. We can multiply the existing area of the shape by this ASF to find the new area:
$8 \times 4 = 32$
The new area of the shape is 32cm².

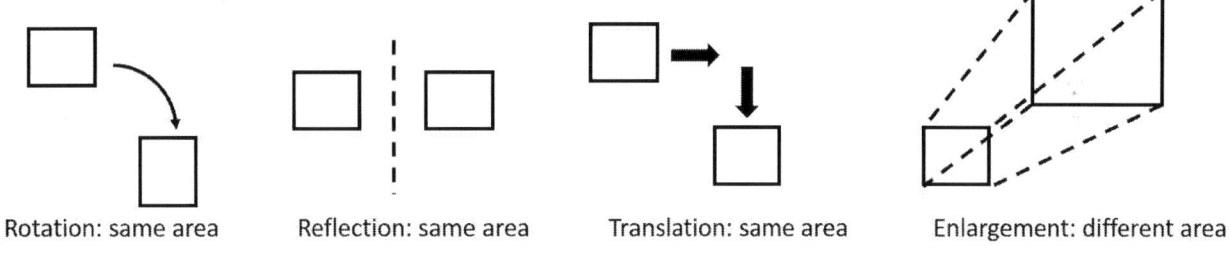

Rotation: same area   Reflection: same area   Translation: same area   Enlargement: different area

8

We will use several circle theorems to find the angle AFE.
The reflex angle at O will be:
$360° - 40° = 320°$
The reflex angle at O is 320°.
The angle at the centre is twice the angle at the circumference, so we can find angle ACB:
$\frac{320°}{2} = 160°$
Angle $ACB = 160°$
ACD is a straight line so we can find angle BCD:
$180° - 160° = 20°$
Angle BCD is 20°.

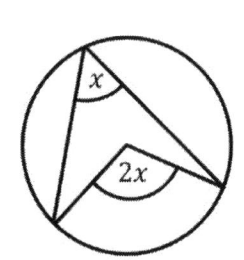

Angle at the centre equals twice the angle at the circumference:
Circumference angle is x.
Centre angle is $2x$.

Geometry Solutions

Using alternate angles (a "Z" shape), we can find angle ADE.
Angle BCD is the same as angle ADE, so angle ADE is 20°.
We can now use angles in the same segment to find the angle AFE.
Angle ADE and angle AFE are in the same segment which means they are equal.
Therefore angle $AFE = 20°$.

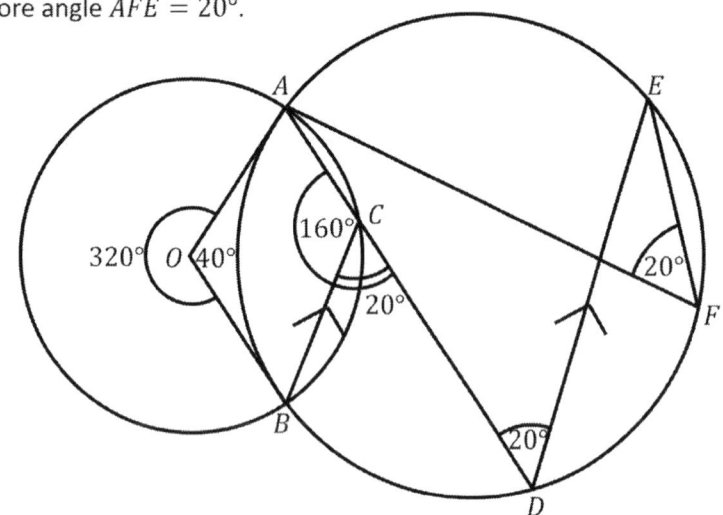

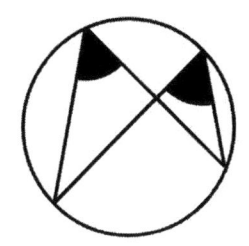

Angles in the same segment: The shaded angles are equal.

9

We can calculate the area of each triangle using the sine area formula:
$$area = \frac{1}{2} ab \sin C$$
where a and b are the sides next to the angle, C.
You can use the sine area formula when you have an angle sandwiched between two sides.

The area of Triangle A:
$$area = \frac{1}{2} ab \sin C$$
$$= \frac{1}{2} \times 3 \times 3 \times \sin 120°$$
$$= \frac{9}{2} \times \frac{\sqrt{3}}{2}$$
$$= \frac{9\sqrt{3}}{4}$$

The area of Triangle B:
$$area = \frac{1}{2} ab \sin C$$
$$= \frac{1}{2} \times 3 \times 3 \times \sin 60°$$
$$= \frac{9}{2} \times \frac{\sqrt{3}}{2}$$
$$= \frac{9\sqrt{3}}{4}$$

The sine graph is symmetrical about 90°

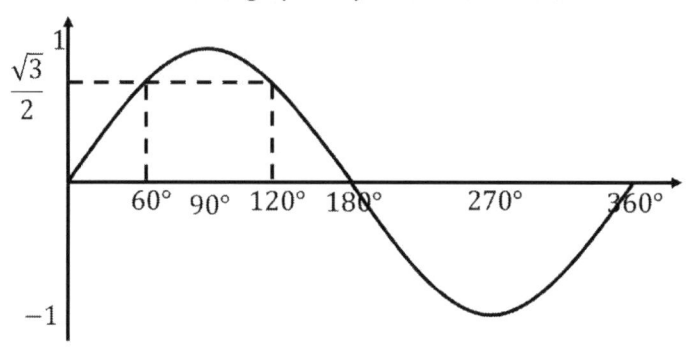

Both triangles have the same area.
The student is incorrect.
The reason that both triangles have the same area is because $\sin 60° = \sin 120°$ as shown in the graph.

GCSE Mathematics 9 – 1

10

With a depth of liquid/ time graph we must use the gradient of the graph to deduce the type of shape that the container being filled has.

When the gradient is constant the shape will be similar to a prism (the cross-sectional area is constant).

When the gradient is increasing it means that the shape is narrowing since the depth is increasing at a greater rate (if the gradient is decreasing it means the shape is getting wider).

From the graph we can see that the gradient starts constant and then gets steeper. This means the object could have a shape like the ones shown.

There are a huge number of potential answers to this problem.

The main points are that the lower part of the shape has a constant cross section and the upper part of the shape has a narrowing cross section.

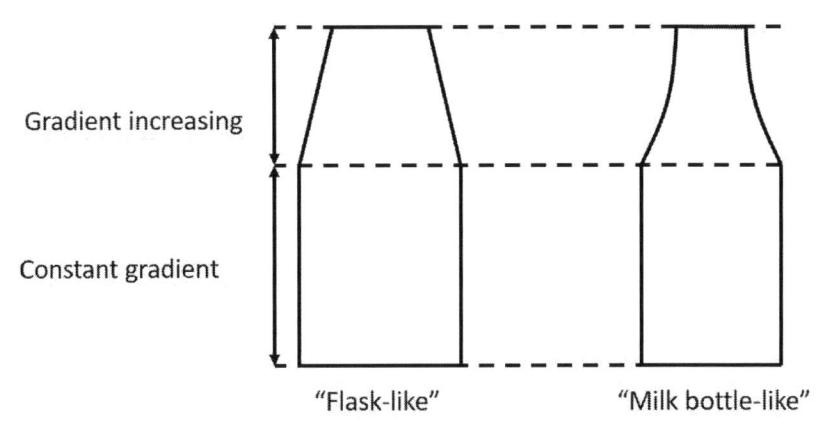

Gradient increasing

Constant gradient

"Flask-like"   "Milk bottle-like"

11

This is a scale factor question involving the volume scale factor (VSF), the area scale factor (ASF) and the length scale factor (LSF).

All cubes are similar, so we can apply these scale factors to find volumes, areas and lengths.

If the volume has reduced by 40% then 60% is remaining. This means the VSF was 0.6.

We can relate the VSF and LSF together:

$volume\ scale\ factor = length\ scale\ factor^3$
$$VSF = LSF^3$$

$LSF^3 = 0.6$
$LSF = \sqrt[3]{0.6}$

We do not need to write a decimal value at this stage.

We can relate the ASF and the LSF together:

$area\ scale\ factor = length\ scale\ factor^2$
$$ASF = LSF^2$$
$$= \left(\sqrt[3]{0.6}\right)^2$$
$$= 0.71137866$$

This effectively tells us that the percentage of surface area remaining would be 71.1% to one decimal place.

The question wanted the percentage reduction which will be given by:

$100 - 71.1 = 28.9\%$

To the nearest percentage, the surface area is reduced by 29%.

12

The triangle ABC is not necessarily right-angled so we will need to use the sine area formula to find its area:

$area = \frac{1}{2}ab \sin C$

a and b are the adjacent sides to the angle C.

We know the sides AB and AC so we can try and find the angle CAB to use in the sine area formula.

Geometry Solutions

To find angle CAB we need to find the side BC. This is because you must know three things about a triangle before you can find other information (excluding three angles).

BC is a side of the isosceles trapezium. Isosceles trapezia are symmetrical about a vertical axis. This means we can form a right-angled triangle with two perpendicular sides of 4cm and 3cm. We can then use Pythagoras to find the side BC:

$a^2 + b^2 = c^2$
$3^2 + 4^2 = BC^2$
$9 + 16 = BC^2$
$BC^2 = 25$
$BC = 5$

We now know all three sides of the triangle ABC.
When you know three sides of a triangle and require one of the interior angles, you need to use the cosine rule:
$a^2 = b^2 + c^2 - 2bc \cos A$

We can rearrange this formula to make $\cos A$ the subject since this is the angle we need. Note that A in this formula is the same as the angle CAB referred to earlier:

$a^2 - b^2 - c^2 = -2bc \cos A$
$\dfrac{a^2 - b^2 - c^2}{-2bc} = \cos A$

Now we can substitute all the sides into the formula with $a = 5, b = 6$ and $c = 5$:

$\cos A = \dfrac{5^2 - 6^2 - 5^2}{-2 \times 6 \times 5}$
$= \dfrac{-36}{-60}$
$= \dfrac{3}{5}$
$A = \cos^{-1} \dfrac{3}{5}$

The angle $CAB = \cos^{-1} \dfrac{3}{5}$.
Leave the angle in this form for now.

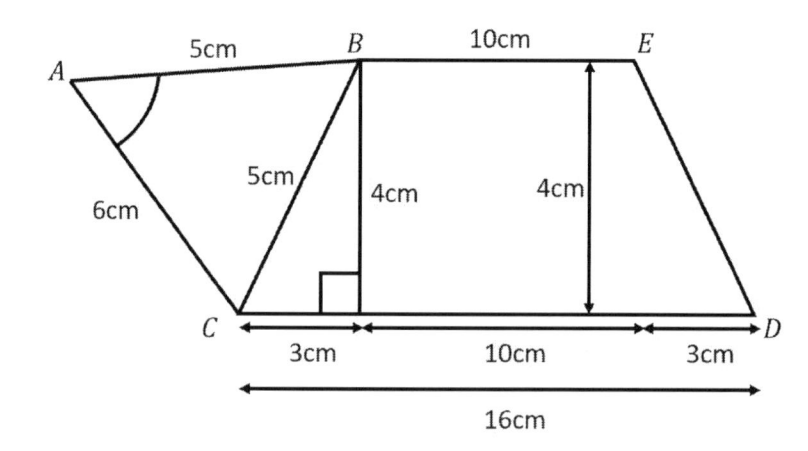

Now we have enough information to use the sine area formula:

$area = \dfrac{1}{2} ab \sin C$
$= \dfrac{1}{2} \times 5 \times 6 \times \sin\left(\cos^{-1} \dfrac{3}{5}\right)$
$= 15 \times 0.8$
$= 12$

Note that C in this generic formula was referring to angle A or angle CAB from before.
The area of triangle ABC is 12cm².
You could have used any angle in triangle ABC so there are other methods that would give you the same answer.

13

The angle between the polygons, 38°, is formed from the exterior angles of both Polygon A and Polygon B added together.
We know that the exterior angle of one polygon is 2° more than the other.
If we let Polygon A have an exterior angle of $x°$ then Polygon B will have an exterior angle of $(x + 2)°$.
The sum of these angles is 38°. This allows us to form an equation and solve for x:

$x + x + 2 = 38°$
$\quad 2x + 2 = 38°$ Collect the terms.
$\quad\quad 2x = 36°$ Subtract 2.
$\quad\quad\quad x = 18°$ Divide by 2.
One of the exterior angles is 18° and the other is 20°.

For the given polygons, the sum of all exterior angles will be 360°. If the polygon is regular, as these two polygons are, then we can divide 360° by the exterior angle to find the number of sides.

$\dfrac{360}{18} = 20 \quad \dfrac{360}{20} = 18$

Polygon A has 18 sides.
Polygon B has 20 sides.
The selection of each polygon could have been done in reverse since the diagram was not to any scale. You could say Polygon A has 20 sides and Polygon B has 18 sides, that would also be a valid answer.

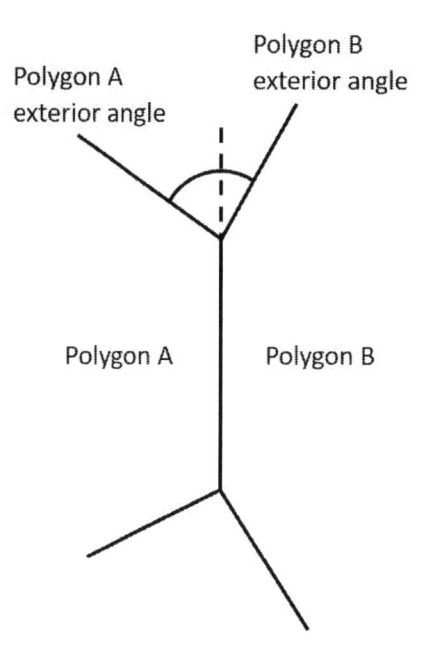

14

We need to draw a diagram to model the directions given in the question:
We can see that the distance between A and B is the hypotenuse of a triangle. The perpendicular sides are 8 and 16 miles.
We now use Pythagoras to find the distance between AB which we will call d:

$a^2 + b^2 = c^2$
$8^2 + 16^2 = d^2$
$d^2 = 64 + 256$
$\quad\; = 320$
$d = 17.9$

The distance between the start points A and B is 17.9 miles correct to three significant figures.

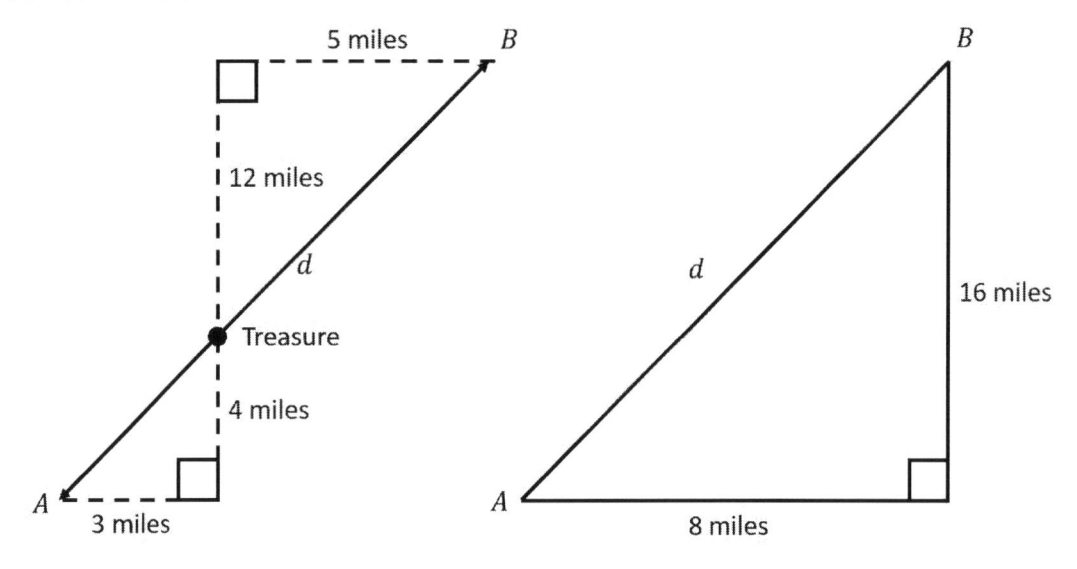

15

If a triangle is right-angled, then Pythagoras must correctly relate all the sides:
$a^2 + b^2 = c^2$
Since the sides of the triangle are also the diameters of the semicircles, we can find these diameters given the areas.

Geometry Solutions

The area of a semicircle is given by:
$$area = \frac{\pi r^2}{2}$$
For the side AC:
$$\frac{\pi r^2}{2} = 18\pi$$
$\frac{r^2}{2} = 18$ Divide by π.
$r^2 = 36$ Multiply by 2.
$r = 6$ Square root.

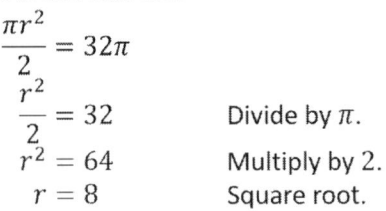

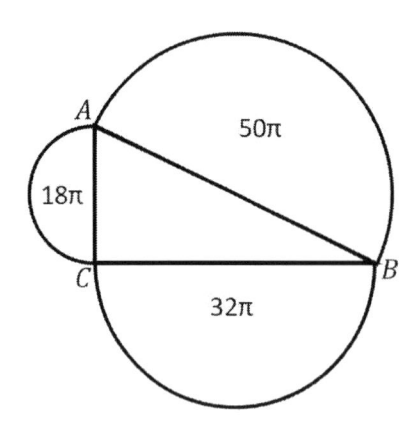

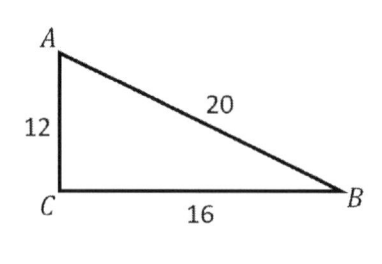

For the side CB:
$$\frac{\pi r^2}{2} = 32\pi$$
$\frac{r^2}{2} = 32$ Divide by π.
$r^2 = 64$ Multiply by 2.
$r = 8$ Square root.

For the side AB:
$$\frac{\pi r^2}{2} = 50\pi$$
$\frac{r^2}{2} = 50$ Divide by π.
$r^2 = 100$ Multiply by 2.
$r = 10$ Square root.

The three sides (diameters) are 12, 16 and 20.
The sum of the squares of the two smaller sides will be:
$a^2 + b^2 = 12^2 + 16^2$
          $= 144 + 256$
          $= 400$

The square of the longer side will be:
$c^2 = 20^2$
    $= 400$

Since $a^2 + b^2 = c^2$ we conclude that the triangle is right-angled.

16

We need to draw a diagram to model the information in the question:
Call the distance from where the balloon is now to the start point a.
The balloon changed from a southeast bearing to a west bearing. This would form a 45° angle between the directions as shown in the diagram.
We have formed a triangle with an angle sandwiched between two sides. We require the side length opposite the angle which means we can use the cosine rule:

$a^2 = b^2 + c^2 - 2bc \cos A$
$= 5^2 + \left(\dfrac{10}{\sqrt{2}}\right)^2 - 2 \times 5 \times \dfrac{10}{\sqrt{2}} \times \cos 45°$
$= 25 + 50 - \dfrac{100}{\sqrt{2}} \times \dfrac{1}{\sqrt{2}}$
$= 75 - 50$
$= 25$
$a = 5$

The balloon is 5 miles from the starting position.

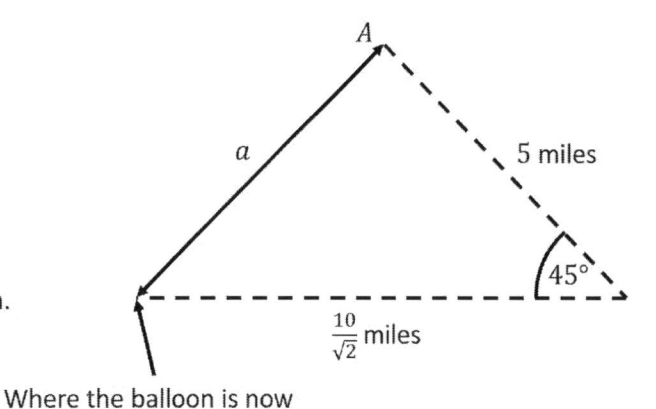

Cosine rule

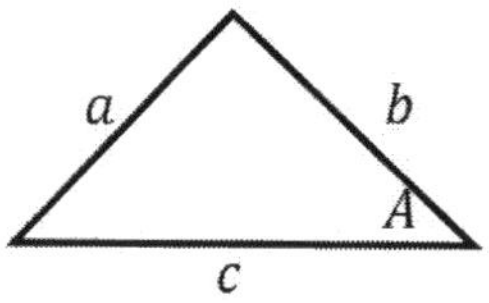

17

The area of a segment can be found using the following formula:
$area\ of\ segment = area\ of\ sector - area\ of\ triangle$
$\qquad\qquad\qquad\quad = area\ of\ sector\ ODB - area\ of\ triangle\ ODB$

To find the area of sector ODB and the triangle ODB we will need the radius of the circle and the angle DOB.
We already know the radius is 1cm.
The angle DOB can be found by using the "alternate segment theorem". The angle $EBC = 15°$, by the alternate segment theorem we can say that angle $BDO = 15°$.
The triangle ODB is isosceles since two of its sides are the radii of the circle.
The angle DOB can be found as follows:
$angle\ DOB = 180° - 15° - 15°$
$\qquad\qquad\quad = 150°$

Now we can use the formula from above to find the area of the segment.
The area of a triangle can be found using $area = \dfrac{1}{2} ab \sin C$ where a and b are the adjacent sides to the angle C.
The area of a sector can be found by:
$area\ of\ sector = \dfrac{angle\ of\ sector}{360°} \times \pi r^2$

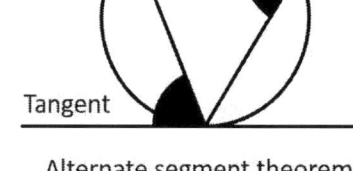

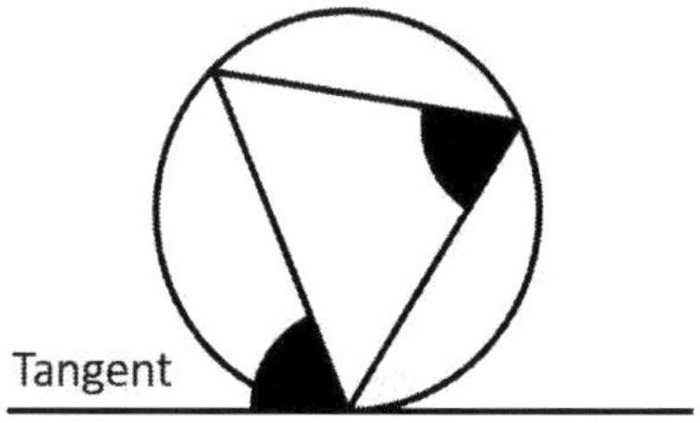

The area of the segment will be:

$area\ of\ segment = area\ of\ sector\ ODB - area\ of\ triangle\ ODB$
$\qquad\qquad\qquad = \dfrac{angle\ of\ sector\ ODB}{360°} \times \pi r^2 - \dfrac{1}{2} ab \sin C$
$\qquad\qquad\qquad = \dfrac{150°}{360°} \times \pi \times 1^2 - \dfrac{1}{2} \times 1 \times 1 \times \sin 150°$
$\qquad\qquad\qquad = \dfrac{5}{12}\pi - \dfrac{1}{2} \times \dfrac{1}{2}$
$\qquad\qquad\qquad = \dfrac{5}{12}\pi - \dfrac{1}{4}$
$\qquad\qquad\qquad = 1.06$

The area of the shaded segment is 1.06cm² to three significant figures.

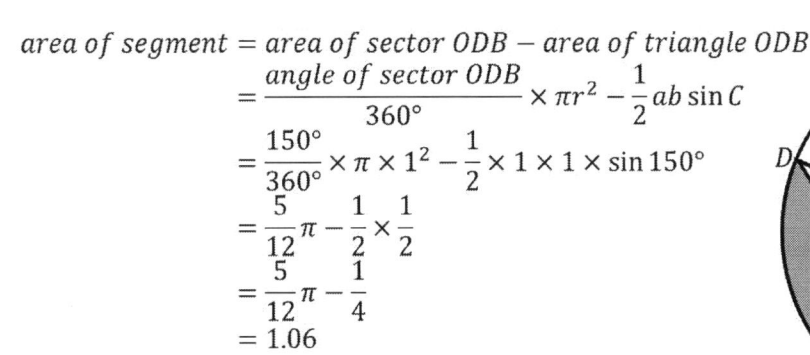

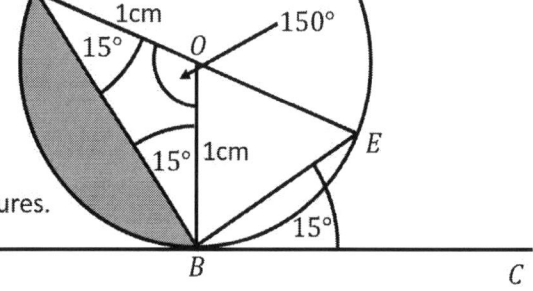

Alternate segment theorem:
The shaded angles are equal.

Geometry Solutions

18

We need to calculate the volume of one pyramid. Then we divide by 0.5 to find how many seconds it would take to empty the pyramid. After that we multiply by 6 since a pyramid was emptied that many times. We then need to find how long after 12:00 noon this is.
The base area is a square which can be found by squaring the side length.
The volume of the pyramid is:
$$volume = \frac{1}{3} \times base\ area \times height$$
$$= \frac{1}{3} \times 8^2 \times 12$$
$$= 256$$
A single pyramid has a volume of 256cm³.
We now divide this by 0.5:
$$\frac{256}{0.5} = 512$$
One pyramid takes 512 seconds to empty. If this was repeated six times the total time will be:
$$6 \times 512 = 3072$$
Six pyramids take 3,072 seconds to empty.
The answer must be given in minutes so we divide by 60:
$$\frac{3072}{60} = 51.2$$
The time for six pyramids to empty is 51.2 minutes, which will be 51 minutes to the nearest minute.
The time will be 12:51pm.

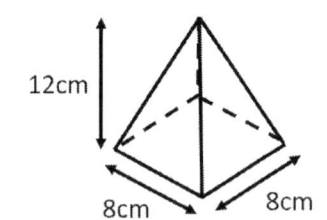

19

For this geometry problem we will require knowledge of:
- Diagonals in a kite cross at right-angles
- The diagonals in a kite can form similar triangles
- Trigonometry SOHCAHTOA

Notice that the triangle ABD is a right-angled triangle. This means we can find the side BD using Pythagoras:
$$a^2 + b^2 = c^2$$
$$AB^2 + AD^2 = BD^2$$
$$5^2 + 12^2 = BD^2$$
$$25 + 144 = BD^2$$
$$BD^2 = 169$$
$$BD = 13$$
Now we need to look at the similar triangles AXD and ABX.
Angle AXD and angle AXB are both equal and 90°
because the diagonals in a kite cross at right-angles.
Let angle $ADX = x$.
Then for angle DAX:
$$angle\ DAX = 180° - 90° - x$$
$$= 90° - x$$
For angle BAX:
$$angle\ BAX = 90° - (90° - x)$$
$$= 90° - 90° + x$$
$$= x$$

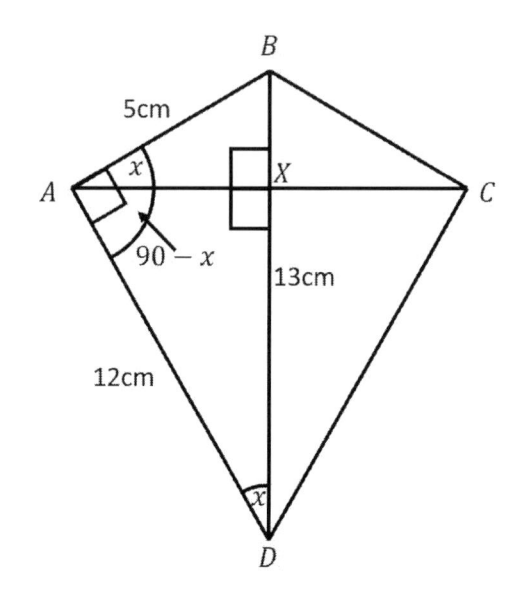

GCSE Mathematics 9 – 1

We can now use trigonometry (SOHCAHTOA) on the triangles AXD and ABX to find the lengths of the sides BX and DX.

If we look at triangle AXD and use SOHCAHTOA:
$$\cos x = \frac{adjacent}{hypotenuse}$$
$$= \frac{DX}{12}$$
$$DX = 12\cos x$$

But we know the exact value of $\cos x$ since for the triangle ABD we know all the sides. This means that we can write the exact value of $\cos x$ in terms of triangle ABD:
$$\cos x = \frac{adjacent}{hypotenuse}$$
$$= \frac{12}{13}$$

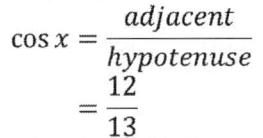

We can substitute this value into the equation for DX:
$$DX = 12\cos x$$
$$= 12\left(\frac{12}{13}\right)$$
$$= \frac{144}{13}$$

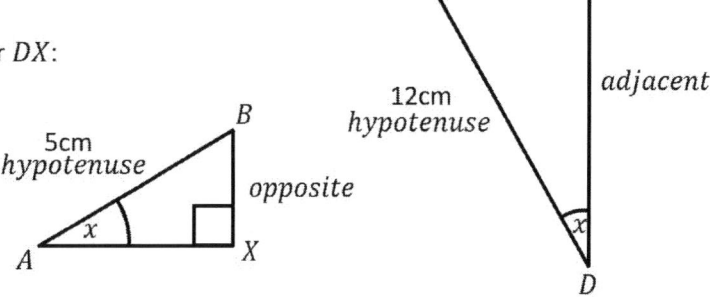

If we look at triangle ABX and use SOHCAHTOA:
$$\sin x = \frac{opposite}{hypotenuse}$$
$$= \frac{BX}{AB}$$
$$= \frac{BX}{5}$$
$$BX = 5\sin x$$

But we know the exact value of $\sin x$ since for the triangle ABD we know all the sides.

This means that we can write the exact value of $\sin x$ in terms of triangle ABD:
$$\sin x = \frac{opposite}{hypotenuse}$$
$$= \frac{5}{13}$$

We can substitute this value into the equation for BX:
$$BX = 5\sin x$$
$$= 5\left(\frac{5}{13}\right)$$
$$= \frac{25}{13}$$

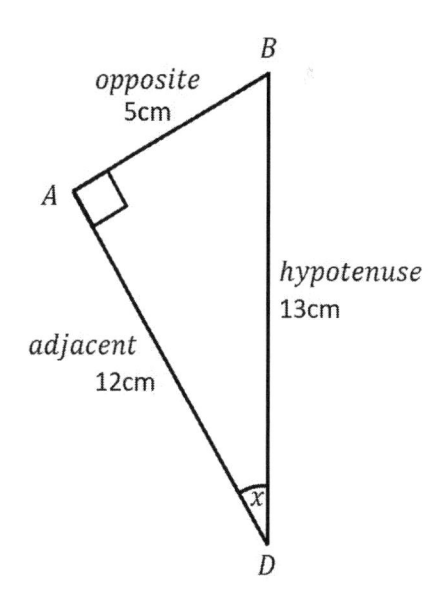

We can now answer the question by dividing the length of DX by BX:
$$\frac{DX}{BX} = \frac{\frac{144}{13}}{\frac{25}{13}} \qquad \text{Both fractions have a denominator of 13, this means they cancel out.}$$
$$= \frac{144}{25}$$
$$= 5.76$$

Geometry Solutions

The side DX is 5.76 times longer than the side BX.

20

If the triangular prism occupies a quarter of the entire volume of the cuboid then the surface area of the triangle must also be a quarter that of the cuboid.
The area of the cross-sectional face of the cuboid will be:
$$area\ of\ cross-sectional\ face = 9 \times 4\sqrt{3}$$
$$= 36\sqrt{3}$$
The cross-sectional face has an area of $36\sqrt{3}cm^2$.
The triangle will have an area which is a quarter of this:
$$\frac{36\sqrt{3}}{4} = 9\sqrt{3}$$
The area of the equilateral triangle is $9\sqrt{3}cm^2$.

The area of a triangle can be found using $area = \frac{1}{2}ab\sin C$ where a and b are the adjacent sides to the angle C. In this case sides a and b will be equal and the angle C will be $60°$. If we let the unknown side length be x we can form an equation:
$$\frac{1}{2}ab\sin C = 9\sqrt{3}$$
$$\frac{1}{2} \times x \times x \times \sin 60° = 9\sqrt{3}$$
$$\frac{1}{2}x^2 \times \frac{\sqrt{3}}{2} = 9\sqrt{3}$$
$$\frac{\sqrt{3}x^2}{4} = 9\sqrt{3}$$
$$\frac{x^2}{4} = 9 \qquad \text{Divide by } \sqrt{3}$$
$$x^2 = 36 \qquad \text{Multiply by 4}$$
$$x = 6 \qquad \text{Square root.}$$
The side length of the equilateral triangle is 6cm.

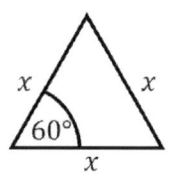

21

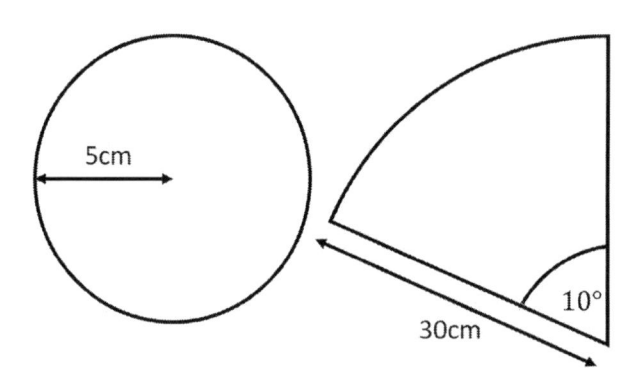

The area of a circle is given by:
$area = \pi r^2$
The area of a sector is given by:
$\frac{angle\ of\ sector}{360} \times \pi r^2$
The areas of these shapes are the same, so we can write an equation to solve for r:

GCSE Mathematics 9 – 1

$area\ of\ circle = area\ of\ sector$

$$\pi \times 5^2 = \frac{10}{360} \times \pi r^2$$

$$25\pi = \frac{1}{36}\pi r^2$$

$$25 = \frac{r^2}{36}$$ Divide by π.

$$900 = r^2$$ Multiply by 36.

$$r = 30$$ Square root.

The radius of the sector is 30cm.

22

The overall objective for this question is to find the area of the smaller circle and the area of the square. We can then subtract the area of the smaller circle from the area of the square to get the shaded area.
The diameter of the smaller circle is equal to the side length of the square.
The diagonal of the square is equal to the diameter of the larger circle.
We can find the diameter of the larger circle since we know the area:
$area = \pi r^2$
$\pi r^2 = 36\pi$
$r^2 = 36$ Divide by π
$r = 6$ Square root.
The radius of the larger circle is 6cm.
The diameter of the larger circle will be 12cm.

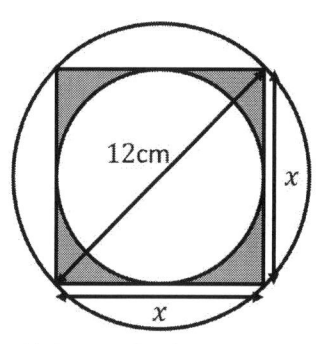

We now use Pythagoras to find the side length of the square. If we let a side of the square be x:
$a^2 + b^2 = c^2$
$x^2 + x^2 = 12^2$
$2x^2 = 144$ Collect the terms.
$x^2 = 72$ Divide by 2.
$x = \sqrt{72}$ Square root.

Leave the answer as $\sqrt{72}$ for now since it is not the final answer.

$\sqrt{72}$cm is also the diameter of the smaller circle, so the radius of the smaller circle will be $\frac{\sqrt{72}}{2}$cm.

The area of the square is $x^2 = 72$cm².
The area of the smaller circle will be:
$area = \pi r^2$
$$= \pi \left(\frac{\sqrt{72}}{2}\right)^2$$
$$= 18\pi$$

The shaded area will be the difference between the square and smaller circle areas:
$shaded\ area = square\ area - small\ circle\ area$
$$= 72 - 18\pi$$
$$= 15.5$$

The shaded area is 15.5cm correct to three significant figures.

23

We know that cubes are similar shapes. This means we can apply scale factors to find the connection between a change in volume and a change in length. We know that the new cube increased in volume by $\frac{61}{64}$; the multiplier for an increase of this would be $1\frac{61}{64}$ or $\frac{125}{64}$.

Geometry Solutions

This multiplier is a volume scale factor (VSF). The VSF is related to the length scale factor (LSF) by the following formula:
$$volume\ scale\ factor = length\ scale\ factor^3$$
$$VSF = LSF^3$$

Since we know the VSF, we can calculate the LSF:
$$LSF^3 = \frac{125}{64}$$
$$LSF = \frac{5}{4}$$

The volume of the larger cube is 1,000cm³. If we cube root this volume we will have the length of one of the sides:
$$\sqrt[3]{1000} = 10$$
The larger cube has a side length of 10cm.
If we divide by the LSF calculated earlier, we will have the side length of the inner limestone:
$$10 \div \frac{5}{4} = 8$$
The side length of the inner limestone cube is 8cm.
The marble covers the limestone evenly so this means there is a 1cm layer of marble either side of the cube.
The depth of marble is 1cm.

24

This question involves scale factors. We need the height h, which is a length. This means we must calculate the length scale factor (LSF) for each cylinder. The question has provided the volume scale factor (VSF) between each cylinder. The formula that connects the VSF and the LSF is given below:
$$VSF = LSF^3$$
We know the volume of Cylinder B is eight times the volume of Cylinder A: $VSF = 8$
$$LSF^3 = 8$$
$$LSF = 2$$
This means the height of Cylinder B will be two times the height of Cylinder A:
$$2 \times 2 = 4$$
The height of Cylinder B is 4cm.

We know the volume of Cylinder C is eight times the volume of Cylinder B: $VSF = 8$
$$LSF^3 = 8$$
$$LSF = 2$$
This means the height of Cylinder C will be two times the height of Cylinder B:
$$4 \times 2 = 8$$
The height of Cylinder C is 8cm.
The total height h is the sum of the cylinder heights:
$$h = 2 + 4 + 8$$
$$= 14$$
The height of the stack is 14cm.

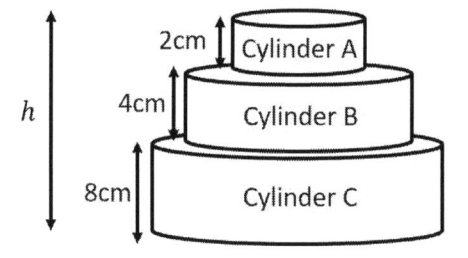

25

We can answer this question by comparing distances in terms of x. We do not necessarily need exact answers for comparison questions, only knowledge of which is larger.
We can form a right-angled triangle that includes Surgery A, the New home and a point on the line connecting Surgery A and Surgery B.
If we can show that the base of this triangle is less than $0.8x$ we know that the New home will be closer to Surgery A. This is because it will be left of the perpendicular bisector of the line connecting Surgery A and Surgery B. Call the base of the right-angled triangle b.

GCSE Mathematics 9 – 1

We will use SOHCAHTOA to find b.
We also know that the angle inside the triangle will be 60°. This is because Surgery B is on a bearing of 100° from Surgery A.

$$\cos 60° = \frac{adjacent}{hypotenuse}$$
$$= \frac{b}{x}$$
$b = x \cos 60°$ $\cos 60° = 0.5$
$ = 0.5x$

Since $0.5x < 0.8x$ we conclude that the distance to Surgery A must be less.

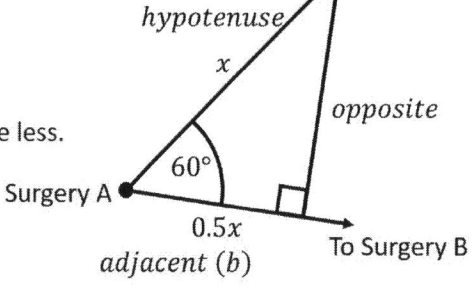

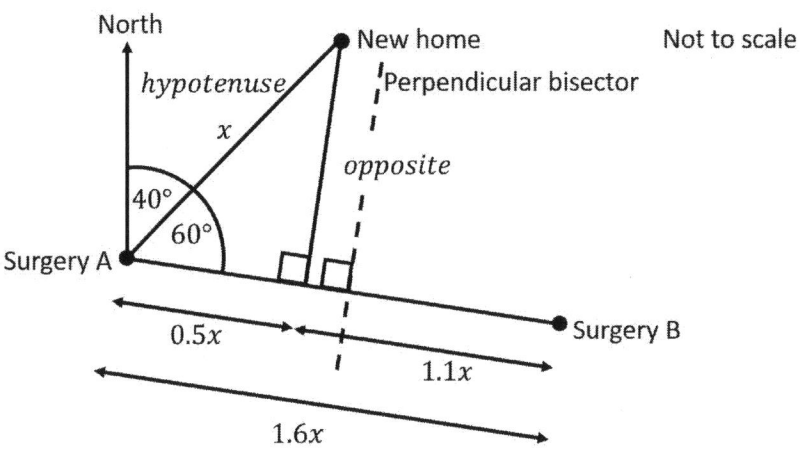

Surgery A is closer.

10 PROBABILITY SOLUTIONS

1

There are several factors of 72 that would lead to a win. As there are multiple options a probability-space table is the best approach to avoid missing any answers. This table will show all outcomes:

×	1	2	3	4	5	6
1	1	2	3	4	5	6
2	2	4	6	8	10	12
3	3	6	9	12	15	18
4	4	8	12	16	20	24
5	5	10	15	20	25	30
6	6	12	18	24	30	36

The factors of 72 shown in the table are:
1,2,3,4,6,8,9,12,18,24,36
The table has dimensions 6×6; this means the probability will be out of 36.
Of the 36 outcomes, 24 of them are factors of 72.
The probability of winning the game is:
$$\frac{24}{36} = \frac{2}{3}$$
The fully simplified answer is $\frac{2}{3}$.

2

We must first calculate the probability of a single candidate being offered a job. For this, the candidate must be invited for interview and then offered a job. Since these are successive events we multiply the probabilities together:
$0.2 \times 0.3 = 0.06$
We can say that the probability of a single candidate being offered a job is 0.06.
For two successive candidates to be offered a job we need to multiply the probability of being offered a job by itself (because this is again, a successive event):
$0.06 \times 0.06 = 0.0036$
The probability of two candidates successively being offered a job at this cyber security firm is 0.0036.

3

Knowing the first and third digits of a four digit code means only the second and fourth digits are required. The actual positioning of the unknown digits is not relevant, only that there are two unknowns to find. Each digit is a selection from 10 different possibilities. This means the probability of correctly guessing one of the unknowns is $\frac{1}{10}$. Both digits must be correctly guessed at the same time (which means in succession). When probabilities are occurring in succession the probabilities are multiplied together. The other unknown digit is selected from 10 different possibilities, so the probability of correctly guessing will be $\frac{1}{10}$.

GCSE Mathematics 9 – 1

The probability of correctly guessing both unknowns will be:
$$\frac{1}{10} \times \frac{1}{10} = \frac{1}{100}$$
The correct answer is $\frac{1}{100}$.
This can also be thought of as there being 100 different two digit numbers that you can form from the digits 0 to 9, of which you require one of the 100.

4

The most important thing to recognise in this question is that of the three styluses, any two of them could break. This means that there will be more than one outcome where two of the three styluses have broken. There are three different pathways:
Break – Break – No Break
Break – No Break – Break
No Break – Break – Break

$\xrightarrow{0.1}$ Break $\xrightarrow{0.1}$ Break $\xrightarrow{0.9}$ No Break $0.1 \times 0.1 \times 0.9 = 0.009$

$\xrightarrow{0.1}$ Break $\xrightarrow{0.9}$ No Break $\xrightarrow{0.1}$ Break $0.1 \times 0.9 \times 0.1 = 0.009$

$\xrightarrow{0.9}$ No Break $\xrightarrow{0.1}$ Break $\xrightarrow{0.1}$ Break $0.9 \times 0.1 \times 0.1 = 0.009$

$$0.009 + 0.009 + 0.009 = 0.027$$

The probability of each pathway is found by multiplying each probability as you progress. This will be done for the three pathways. The probabilities of each pathway are then added to give the overall probability:
The probability of exactly two styluses breaking in the first year is 0.027.

5

This question involves conditional probability.
Consider the days that are below or equal to 10°C first.
There is a probability of 0.8 that a spider will spin a web on each day. If a web is spun there is a probability of 0.7 that a fly is caught. Since these events must occur in succession we multiply the probabilities together:
$0.8 \times 0.7 = 0.56$
There is a probability of 0.56 that the spider will catch a fly on days that are below or equal to 10°C.
Since there were 1,400 days that are below or equal to 10°C, we can multiply the probability of a spider catching a fly by the number of days:
$0.56 \times 1400 = 784$
We estimate 784 days of 1,400 days where the spider catches a fly.
Now consider the days that are above 10°C.
There is a probability of 0.6 that a spider will spin a web on each day. If a web is spun there is a probability of 0.7 that a fly is caught. Since these events must occur in succession we multiply the probabilities together:
$0.6 \times 0.7 = 0.42$

There is a probability of 0.42 that the spider will catch a fly on days that are above 10°C.
Since there were 1,050 days that are above 10°C, we can multiply the probability of a spider catching a fly by the number of days:
$0.42 \times 1050 = 441$
We estimate 441 days of 1,050 days where the spider catches a fly.
The total estimate will be the sum of the estimates:
$784 + 441 = 1225$

Probability Solutions

We estimate that the spider caught a fly on 1,225 days in total.
The total number of days was $1400 + 1050 = 2450$ days.
The percentage of days that we estimate the spider caught a fly on is:
$$\frac{1225}{2450} \times 100 = 50\%$$
The estimate is 50%.

6

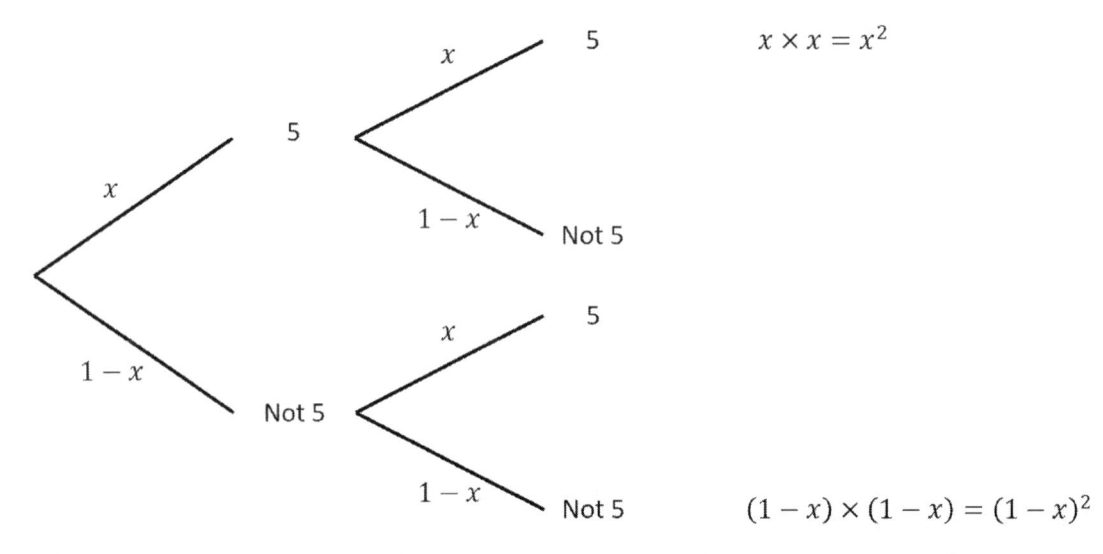

$x \times x = x^2$

$(1-x) \times (1-x) = (1-x)^2$

The probability of each branching in the tree must sum to 1. If the probability of an event is x, the probability of the event not occurring is $1 - x$.
We multiply along the branches of the probability tree to get the outcome probability.
The outcome probabilities are given as a ratio. To form an equation to solve for x, we must cross multiply the ratio and the expressions together:

$x^2 : (1-x)^2$

$9 : 4$

$$9(1-x)^2 = 4x^2$$
$$9(1-x)(1-x) = 4x^2$$
$$9(1-x-x+x^2) = 4x^2 \quad \text{Multiply out.}$$
$$9(1-2x+x^2) = 4x^2$$
$$9 - 18x + 9x^2 = 4x^2 \quad \text{Multiply out.}$$
$$5x^2 - 18x + 9 = 0 \quad \text{Subtract } 4x^2.$$
$$(5x-3)(x-3) = 0 \quad \text{Factorise.}$$ 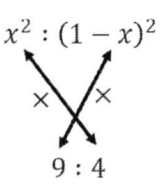
$$5x - 3 = 0$$
$$5x = 3$$
$$x = \frac{3}{5}$$
This is a valid solution.
$$x - 3 = 0$$
$$x = 3$$
This is not valid since x must not be greater than 1 (x is a probability).
The correct answer is $x = \frac{3}{5}$ or $x = 0.6$

7

The most important thing to recognise in this question is that of the four words, any one of them could be the slang word. This means that there will be more than one outcome where one of the four words is slang. There are four different pathways:

Slang – Non-slang – Non-slang – Non-slang
Non-slang – Slang – Non-slang – Non-slang
Non-slang – Non-slang – Slang – Non-slang
Non-slang – Non-slang – Non-slang – Slang

The probability of non-slang will be $1 - 0.12 = 0.88$

$\xrightarrow{0.12}$ Slang $\xrightarrow{0.88}$ Non-slang $\xrightarrow{0.88}$ Non-slang $\xrightarrow{0.88}$ Non-slang

$\xrightarrow{0.88}$ Non-slang $\xrightarrow{0.12}$ Slang $\xrightarrow{0.88}$ Non-slang $\xrightarrow{0.88}$ Non-slang

$\xrightarrow{0.88}$ Non-slang $\xrightarrow{0.88}$ Non-slang $\xrightarrow{0.12}$ Slang $\xrightarrow{0.88}$ Non-slang

$\xrightarrow{0.88}$ Non-slang $\xrightarrow{0.88}$ Non-slang $\xrightarrow{0.88}$ Non-slang $\xrightarrow{0.12}$ Slang

$0.12 \times 0.88 \times 0.88 \times 0.88 = 0.081776644$

$0.88 \times 0.12 \times 0.88 \times 0.88 = 0.081776644$

$0.88 \times 0.88 \times 0.12 \times 0.88 = 0.081776644$

$0.88 \times 0.88 \times 0.88 \times 0.12 = 0.081776644$

$0.081776644 \times 4 = 0.32710656$

The probability of each pathway is found by multiplying each probability as you progress. This will be done for the four pathways. The probabilities of each pathway are then added to give the overall probability:
The probability of selecting four words, one of which is slang is 0.327 correct to three significant figures.

Author.

ABOUT BARTON MATHS TUITION

Barton Maths Tuition provides educational texts for GCSE students. The author is a private maths and science tutor supporting students in the area around Barton Under Needwood, Staffordshire.

Printed in Poland
by Amazon Fulfillment
Poland Sp. z o.o., Wrocław